Experiencing the Grace & Purpose of Pentecost

JOHN KINGSLEY ALLEY

Holy Community, Experiencing the Grace and Purpose of Pentecost
Copyright © 2010 by John Kingsley Alley.

Published by:
Peace Publishing,
Rockhampton, Queensland, Australia.

Distributed in Australia by:
Peace Christian Resources
Locked Bag 8004
Rockhampton Qld 4700
Phone: 07 4922 7055
Email: books@peace.org.au
Web: www.peace.org.au

All rights reserved. No portion of this publication may be reproduced, stored in a retrieval system, or transmitted in any form by any means – electronic, mechanical, photocopying, recording, or any other – except for brief quotations in printed reviews, without the prior written permission of the author.

Unless otherwise indicated, all Scripture quotations are taken from the HOLY BIBLE, NEW INTERNATIONAL VERSION. Copyright 1973, 1978, 1984 by International Bible Society. Used by permission of Zondervan Publishing House. All rights reserved.

Scripture quotations marked KJV are taken from the King James Version of the Bible.

Scripture quotations marked NASB are taken from the NEW AMERICAN STANDARD BIBLE®, Copyright © 1960,1962,1963,1968,1971,1972,1973,1975,1977,1995 by The Lockman Foundation. Used by permission.

ISBN 1-452819-32-7

First Edition - April 2010

Dedication

To the man or woman of God

who will weep before Him,

so as to see the grace here spoken of

find fulfillment in their people.

ACKNOWLEDGEMENTS

I want to express my deep appreciation to the many members of
Peace Apostolic Community
who tirelessly pray for me, and speak often with me
and encourage me with their love,
So many of them, Godly men and women, are diligent in prayer meetings,
and never seem to flag from hope,
and are always finding fresh and encouraging words
from the Holy Spirit for us all.

For my leadership team and office staff, too many to name here,
I am deeply grateful, and I love them.
They are always in prayer for our work
endlessly patient with me, and so supportive,
and love me and each other, and love doing what we do.

I sincerely want to thank those members of the ministry team,
who willingly travel anywhere on short notice or none.
It is wonderful the way you have stuck together as one.

I thank Mrs Bronwyn Batley in particular,
who as a volunteer spent many days over many months
combing through and sorting transcripts of what I have preached,
to give me a ready supply of resource material for writing.

And Jonathan Maxwell, creative genius,
who works as part of our team, and has such an excellent spirit.
Thank you for great designs, and great partnership in the ministry.

I especially want to thank Hazel, my wife,
who spends herself so fully in what we do,
and whose heart is so much in it.
She is great with detail, and has worked harder than anyone,
and has helped me maintain the long hours I spend on so many things.
She goes carefully through what I write, not only to help with accuracy of detail,
but to help me test the spirit of what is written,
so I can hope to keep the errors to a bare minimum.
Hazel has been a great help to me in everything.

HOLY COMMUNITY

CONTENTS

Foreword

By Apostle Chris Peterson

Having been an Assemblies of God minister for over forty years, it has been my privilege to serve as a local church pastor and at various levels of executive church governance & strategic development, during which time the Assemblies of God in Queensland saw explosive growth.

In my experience, one of the perennial issues that confront us in church growth and church planting is the need to build a sustainable and strong community culture.

For over fifteen years I have known of the significant ministry of John Alley. Over the past two years I have developed a meaningful apostolic relationship with him as we have found ourselves on a very similar journey of not only becoming aware of the five-fold and the importance of the apostolic, but coming to a place where we have owned the calling, and begun to engage in apostolic ministry to establish the Kingdom of God in power & significant influence beyond the walls of the church, with a view to transforming society.

In John 13:35 Jesus declared that the ultimate impact on the world is going to come through the manifestation of true Christian community, which is desperately needed in our church environment where casual, superficial and often exploitive relationships have been the order of the day.

Last year, it was my privilege to be invited to be a speaker at John's conference. Having gone to give input to this conference, I was personally impacted by things that transcended the dynamics of meetings, music & preaching. There was a tangible sense of family, of genuine care and a culture of honour and support being outworked at every level. I engaged with many people during the course of the conference and was personally impacted by these tangible values.

It was very interesting and inspiring to see such an emphasis on quality relationship whist at the same time maintaining the passion and faith to pursue a sacrificial commitment to reaching a lost world and establish the Kingdom of God.

Since this conference, and as my relationship with John has grown stronger, it has been my joy to encourage those seeking to develop these values to not only read his material on sonship and community, but also attend his conferences which so powerfully demonstrate the values that they embrace.

It is a great privilege to have established fellowship with John and Peace, and I am personally enriched by it.

Your brother in Christ,

Chris.

Apostle Chris Peterson
ApostleNet International,
ACTS Church International,
Caloundra, Qld, Australia.

Introduction
TO THE MESSAGE
BY DR. JOHN MCELROY

One of the greatest challenges in writing a book on any aspect of the Christian faith is to combine revelatory insight with experiential knowledge. John Alley is an apostolic leader who combines both revelation and experience in his writings. I personally have observed a consistent and empowering grace that is evident in his relationships, both with his family and among his colleagues in ministry.

If I could choose a single Bible verse to describe Peace Ministries, it would be John 13:35, "By this shall all men know that you are my disciples, if you love one another." Whenever I converse with men and women who are spiritual sons and daughters to John and Hazel Alley, I sense a deep passion to embody the Two Great Commandments (Mt. 22:37-40). To see the fruit of this relational passion is a rare and precious experience within the Body of Christ, yet it is very evident within the Peace Community in Rockhampton.

Whenever I read a Christian book, I seek to discover the extent to which the author's insights are based on mere theories or whether they are grounded in experience. Theories always need to be tested. The insights found in John's previous books, *The Apostolic Revelation* and *The Spirit of Sonship*, are powerful because they are actually being lived out.

In Australia, we have a term to express the genuineness of a person or idea, by calling it the 'Real Deal'. John Alley and Peace Ministries are, in my estimation, the 'Real Deal' because they truly embody the apostolic and relational grace that is bringing heaven to earth within the Twenty-first Century Church.

Rev. Dr. John McElroy,
Southern Cross Association of Churches,
Churchlands,
Perth, Western Australia.

Introduction
TO THE AUTHOR
BY JENNY HAGGER AM

When I first met John and Hazel Alley some years ago I was struck by their warmth and openness, and yet I had reservations. Like many of us, I had experienced a few shipwrecked relationships in the Body of Christ, and did not trust myself to once again seek a closer relationship with a spiritual father.

John sensitively detected my resistance. With his gentle and fatherly approach he began to teach me the importance of walking daily in apostolic grace and sonship, while bringing strong correction to me where needed. I was drawn by his love for Christ and his caring heart, not just for me but for my family and the people in the ministries in which I am involved.

His own household of faith is a strong influence in Peace Apostolic Community. John and Hazel with their eight children, extended family of son and daughters-in-law and grandchildren are an incredible witness to the integrity of their ministry. We have seen this first hand when staying in their home or hosting them in Adelaide. There is a sense of peace and order and a flow of grace that has modeled to my husband and me an understanding of the revelations of which John teaches and writes about in his books. These revelations are genuinely outworked in the daily life of his family and community, flowing on to the relating churches and ministries to which John gives apostolic covering.

The love of Christ is clearly seen among his committed leadership team. Their example of walking together in unity enables the ministry to carry an ever-increasing responsibility and influence in the Kingdom of God whether in Australia or overseas. This is the model we desire for our ministries.

It is an honour to be able to share our lives with John and his community, and grow in all that the Father has for us in the coming years.

Jenny Hagger AM
Australian House of Prayer for All Nations,
Mission World Aid,
Zion Hill Christian Community.
Adelaide, South Australia.

Introduction
TO THE MINISTRY
BY APOSTLE CHUCK CLAYTON

I have travelled extensively throughout the United States and abroad, and been in many churches and Pastor's homes. My wife and I have been with Apostle John and Hazel on many occasions in the past several years, and had the privilege of staying in their home, as well as ministering in their church at Rockhampton.

In all honesty, I must say that I have never experienced such a mutual love, honor and respect among a "flock" of people as has touched my life while with them. There has been a Grace for an anointing of peace upon John and Hazel's lives that has definitely permeated the local church at Rockhampton. It is like sitting by a stream that is gently flowing and refreshing everything in its path. The Holy Spirit moves so calmly among the "community" called Peace.

This same quiet presence is in their home as they instruct their children, serve so many people from various nations, and interact in everyday life. To experience a time with their family (natural and spiritual) is to be truly blessed, accepted and loved. They are the closest reflection of Christ and the Church I have yet to see.

My wife once told John and Hazel that she leaves a little piece of her heart with them every time she goes back home.

Apostle Chuck Clayton
Apostolic Resource Ministries,
Dillsboro,Indiana,
United States of America.

Author's INTRODUCTION

It was in seeking to walk with God and bring our people into grace (with years of much prayer in which we were always saying to God, "You can do whatever you wish with us"), that we 'found' the lovely things that have so changed our lives, and of which I here write.

Like a prospector who has found a good, payable, vein of pure gold, but knows there is a mother lode somewhere nearby, we remain hungry and searching for a greater grace – for really there is an even greater grace just beyond the veil, which in many ways still covers our hearts from seeing all of Christ. Otherwise, there would be no need to pray, or for Paul to have written and prayed also, what we find in Ephesians 1:17-19. (And find again in chapter 3:14-19, as well as Colossians 1: 9-12 and 2:1-3)

Holy Community is the companion message to *The Spirit of Sonship*. Both instruct about the grace of the apostolic life of the Church, but each represents a powerful grace in its own right. Because of the possibility of one message overshadowing the other, if combined in one book, I decided two separate books were needed.

One area of teaching, that of sonship and spiritual fathering, focuses on the personal relationships we must walk in with our leaders and each other, and the way this works out in practise. The other, in this book, on what it is like to be whole as a people together – specifically, how the local church can experience a corporate grace, through Pentecost, that causes them to be of one heart. It requires an anointing called "understanding", and creates a common life called "community". These were the terms used by the Lord on those occasions when I was given information about how all this works.

When writing my first book, *The Apostolic Revelation*, I was busy concentrating one day when the Lord spoke, telling me that after I wrote that book, a second level of revelation would come, and then a third. With both *Sonship* and *Community*, we are dealing with that second level He spoke of. But I am now finding light on the third level dawning, too.

At the very outset, can I say plainly, and can I ask you to bear in mind – ***there is a God-given anointing*** for the purpose of building the church as community! That is what I pray each reader of this book will be enabled to take hold of.

It's How We Relate that Counts

Everything we have learned about what it means for believers to be an apostolic people can be summed up in *how we relate* to God, and *how we relate* to each other – and the latter is equally as important as the former, especially if we are to become mature as children of God. If a people has no understanding of how to walk with their leaders and their brethren, this is not an apostolic people, no matter how many people they raise from the dead or how much they prophesy.

Speaking in tongues, healing, and prophecy are great gifts to the Church, but they are in no way proofs of apostolic grace. In the past, we have mistakenly assumed that if you had apostolic grace, then you would have miracles, signs and wonders, and gifts; but we missed something very important. Having miracles or gifts of the Spirit is an external manifestation of the Spirit, but it is not proof of what is on the inside. True apostolic grace produces an inner life.

An Apostolic Life

Did the apostle Paul have an inner life by which he not only knew the Lord, but loved the churches? Did Peter also have this inner life by which he loved the brethren? Were those men not willing to lay down their lives for the brethren? The answer, of course, to all these questions, is 'yes.' That is the proof of apostolic grace. Unless we ourselves have the heart that genuinely walks in relationship with others, we are not really living in apostolic grace.

It is not merely a matter of deciding to receive apostles and then changing the structure of the Church to give them a place. Rather, at the heart of true apostolic Christianity are specific attitudes, values, and heart relationships. These values are what determine whether a group of people are apostolic or not.

I look forward to the day when the Church is so filled with apostolic grace that we no longer need to use the term. Meanwhile, when we do use the term 'apostolic,' we are referring to a certain type of Christianity which is the genuine, New Testament, Christ-given article. This is the type of Christianity that produces a life in the people of God that does not depend on institutions or programmes; the people are knit together as one holy people. This is the life that the early apostles gave to the Church. Today, the Church needs to find that life in a fresh way.

Compelling but not Comfortable

One of the things we discovered about having apostolic grace and apostolic anointings upon the church is that even though it's exciting in the sense that the vision is captivating and the purpose so compelling, it does not always make people feel comfortable. I was greeted at the door of our church one Sunday by a sister who made this very observation. She said, "John, this apostolic message and all the changes it has brought feels really right and good, and it is so obvious it is the Lord and what He wants; but even though it feels right, it doesn't leave us feeling comfortable." I would have to think that is always God's way, when He is taking us somewhere.

Letters of Affirmation and Testimony

At the front of this book are four letters of affirmation by significant, well-known, international, apostolic leaders. At the back I have included an Addendum comprised of a number of letters of testimony from members of my own congregation at Peace in Rockhampton.

There is a reason. Both Christ and Paul quote the Scripture that says, *"every matter must be established by the testimony of two or three witnesses."* In particular, I did not want to write the story about what has happened in our church, and the doctrine I hold concerning it, and not have the witness from outside Christian leaders, as well as participating members, to confirm the truth of what I have written about the spirit of our people. I cannot declare that something has happened amongst us, or that it has a certain meaning, and remain credible, unless my own people can also say, from the heart, that it is true. I also asked for those in public ministry who have visited us to bear witness.

Printed below is what I wrote to each of them. I want the reader to know that I would prefer to understate rather than overstate the level of blessing we have, and I tried to ensure that anyone providing a witness was not encouraged to say anything that was hollow for the purpose of promotion. Here is what I wrote in asking for their witness:

> *I was wondering if you would be able to help me. What I am looking for is a short statement, perhaps a few paragraphs, saying how you feel about the validity of our lives, and in particular the validity of our church at home. I am not asking you to 'gild the lily' in any way, but just say what you do see or feel. Are we genuine in grace, are we 'real', what is the atmosphere, is love present, etc. I really didn't want to publish on this subject without perhaps 2 or 3 mature ministries stating they know us and can commend us, if possible.*
>
> *I don't know how you see us exactly, and I am not asking for any undeserved promotional compliments, but rather your own sense of what you have seen or felt about us. I think I need the '2 or 3' witnesses to say we are OK, if I am to speak of Pentecostal grace to the Body of Christ. I am not asking for a commendation of the book itself, but rather of us as a people, if deserved in your view.*

Some of what was written in reply I thought was unprintable, in the sense that it commended us too strongly, and I thought it might be misunderstood and do more harm than good. What was I to do? My wife Hazel reminded me of something we have realised for a while now – it is not us (I know how ordinary and faulty we are) that cause people to feel the love, or peace, or Christ-likeness at all – it is that there is an anointing present that provides a grace. This is what makes people feel the way they do. I say this to do two things – to point you to Christ whose anointing it is, and to direct you to the very real fact that this anointing is quite freely available for us all in these great days. That's why I felt compelled to write the book.

I commend to you the building of the church of Jesus Christ as a Holy Community.

John Alley,
Peace Apostolic Community,
Rockhampton,
QLD, Australia.

CHAPTER-ONE

THE NEED TO *See*

"I pray also that the eyes of your heart may be enlightened in order that you may know the hope to which he has called you, the riches of his glorious inheritance in the saints, and his incomparably great power for us who believe."

Ephesians 3: 18-19a

The word *community* is not one that everyone relates to. For some it has unwanted associated ideas, and for me it was too weak for use as a 'flagship' for the ministry. But this was the word the Lord used when giving me critical information in answer to our prayers about the life of the church, and what we were looking for in Him.

And to avoid misunderstanding, let us clear up a

common misconception. We are not talking about living in a commune, or the church sharing in some kind of vegetable pool, or well-off believers putting tyres on the car of those poorer. You can do all this if you wish, but it won't give you community in the New Testament sense of what God wants to do with us.

What we are speaking of is the change, through grace, that God can make in the heart of a people that will totally shift the way they *see* each other – and in a single act God the Holy Spirit can do this for a local church corporately. I cannot guarantee that every last individual sitting there becomes the beneficiary of this, but the church as a whole certainly does.

There can be difficulty in getting people to see that this is real – or that it might be different to what they already have. This requires eyes to be opened to see something not visible; and very often, eyes don't want to be opened. We are easily locked in to the assumptions of the spiritual climate and culture we have known, with no great anticipation of things working differently from the experience of life we have had – and thus we interpret what we hear through the grid of our established expectations.

A close associate was with me while I was conducting our School of Apostolic Ministry. I had alluded to community and built it into everything else we had done for several days. Finally, there was a session when I seemed to really get a powerful grip on it. At the end of that session my friend remarked that it was the first time I had ever preached that message. I replied, "I have shared this with the church for years, and you were with me in a conference a few months ago where I taught two whole sessions on it. And you were with me in the Philippines where I taught this everywhere we went."

That illustrates how difficult it can be to really see beyond what we think we know. May I assure you, there is a secret for transforming the life of the church – but it may be so similar, at least in theory, to what we have or think we have, that we might easily gloss over it. Yet it remains a very real and powerful thing on another level altogether from what we have generally walked in.

I will use part of my own story to illustrate. When I was 21, I read a couple of books – *Prison to Praise* by Merlin Carothers, and then *Nine O'clock in the Morning* by Dennis Bennett – that awoke me to the baptism of the Spirit in a new way and made me very hungry. Earlier, I had been powerfully converted when I was 15, and had learned what it meant to be filled with the Holy Spirit by the time I was 16. I also began preaching at that time. In the years between my conversion and reading those books, I was devoted as a disciple and servant of Christ, I was prayerful, lived a holy life, and witnessed to perhaps hundreds of people.

I had been raised in an environment where teaching on the fullness of the Holy Spirit and living a life of holiness was daily bread. The belief that you could wait upon God and be endued with power from above so as to live a holy life with power to win souls, was normal. Yet when I read those books I discovered there was more to the baptism of the Spirit than I had ever understood – and I became determined to obtain what was available.

Thus I began a process of prayer, and for five days remained in the spirit of prayer, my heart crying out to God, looking for this baptism of the Spirit. There was for me a tension between the idea of praying and then going out in faith believing you had received it, as against staying there until you got a breakthrough experience. I just knew there was something here that was real and big, and I had to find it. So I kept praying for it as if I didn't yet have it, but all the while having to face this challenge of coming to the place of believing 'I receive it now'. And by the fifth night I was desperate enough that I just had to believe.

There came a point late that evening when I decided in my own heart that if believing was the key, and if opening my mouth and speaking in tongues by faith was part of the key, this was the thing I had to do. So I decided the moment had come to stand, open my mouth and begin to speak, but not speak any English – and do this as a step of faith. And that's what I did. The moment I started to make a sound I was flooded with grace, touched by the power of the Holy Spirit, and a new language burst forth in rapid torrents.

I had found something of another dimension in Christ. My life testified to it. I had power before, but the dimension of power I now stepped into was totally other than what I had known. There was an amazing outcome in understanding the Scriptures, worship, in exercise of authority, in answers to prayer, and of power in winning souls. But there was more. My life had been transformed and my heart healed when at 15 I had been profoundly converted. Yet the healing of the heart that took place when I was 21 was astounding in other ways, and it seemed an even more sovereign act of God than on the previous occasion.

What I had discovered, of course, was that there was more of the Holy Spirit, but on another level. And I use this here to illustrate that, in another area of life requiring the help and intervention of the Holy Spirit– that of corporate church life, where each believer needs to be in dynamic relationship with other believers – ***there is another level entirely to what most of us have known***, and it is a *grace and power* level.

One of my tasks is to show that, for the purpose of building our people together, we are dealing with a power issue. For if you do not find this thing we call *community* as an outcome of an anointing being given, you won't actually have the grace and power at work which is available to transform church life. That leaves only the inherent gifts of leaders, and the varying goodwill and co-operation of individual believers to build the house of God. No wonder so many struggle.

At 16 I had been given a great book about the full blessing of Pentecost. I had read that book too, and prayed to be filled with the Holy Spirit, and had others pray for me as well. In our terms, and by our light, I had the full blessing of Pentecost – only to discover five years later that Pentecost was surely bigger – i.e. bigger than what we had been thinking.

How is it that over a period of five or six years you can pray repeatedly for the full blessing of Pentecost, as we did, but only seem to get the measure that you know about? That is, in fact, what does happen. We tend to get what we believe for. When we believe something is available, we seem to be able to take hold of it.

Just as I had to move on personally from that more basic understanding of being filled with the Holy Spirit, to see a bigger Pentecost so as to find a greater grace, so does the whole church need to 'see' an even more powerful Pentecost that can transform its corporate life with power, taking the fellowship of the saints to another place. There are greater anointings, and they are worth finding.

This Brings Us to Another Great Need

There is something the Bible teaches which, I think, is largely overlooked. Though of supreme importance – I think it is both primary and central to Christian identity and church life – during the more than 40 years in which I have heard much wonderful teaching from great Christian leaders, I don't think it has been really set before the church.

Yet the Lord is giving us light on many things we have not looked at closely, or closely enough. True, there is nothing new under the sun, but God is giving us grace to walk in some things in the New Testament previously glossed over. Of course we knew it was the truth, but it was not part of our experience – and neither did it seem possible that it would be. Possibly we accepted it as a truth for ourselves personally, but we did not see it as truth that must change the church.

That brings up the question of unbelief. Someone has said that unbelief occurs in us when we know that something in the world around us is contrary to the will of God, but just accept that it can't be changed. 1 Corinthians 1:10 is a great example of this kind of unbelief showing up in church life:

> *"I appeal to you, brothers, in the name of Jesus Christ, that all of you agree with one another so that there may be no divisions among you and that you may be perfectly united in mind and thought."*

We have always read this verse as a beauteous thing, but we read on with no concept of how this should actually work out in the Church and no real anticipation of it actually coming to fruition.

On occasion we might read of some revival and long for revival in our own church or nation, but with no actual plan for how we should act or believe to bring this about. So we go blithely on our way, accepting the status quo, while divisions remain in the church. Most Christians living in most streets of most cities have no communication or relationship with other Christians living in their own street. We are therefore in unbelief with respect to the Scriptures.

Not only so, but a veil is over our minds so that we see neither the depth nor the intent of the Scriptures. Yet these words are still the apostle's cry. He was not merely describing the blissful state of fellowship in heaven; he was appealing to the Church to maintain first principles. This was the way it was supposed to be, on a daily basis, in the church in their city.

Even though this is such an important verse, not many will know in which book of the Bible it is found. How unfamiliar we are with our subject! Usually we will read it and like it; it even touches our hearts; but we pass on without any special commitment to it, or recollection of it: it didn't mean enough.

Let's go back to that verse and think about it. *"I appeal to you brothers..."* is an apostolic appeal. In Paul's cry it is apparent that the brothers already knew the truth, and Paul was appealing to them to move their hearts to do something about what they already knew.

"...in the name of Jesus Christ, that all of you agree with one another." This seems a 'tall order' to us, for Paul did not

leave anybody out – *all* should agree, not just some of them. In our human condition, our fallen-yet-redeemed state, how are we to achieve this level of agreement? When we read such a verse, our thinking is coloured by our life experience of growing up in families and in churches – which is why we are in unbelief.

Deep in the human heart, many assumptions exist of which we are not fully conscious. Our belief system, based on our many experiences, tells us it is not possible to have this level of agreement between people. And Satan, actively at work through religious spirits in many believers, will even vocalise opposition to it, saying it is 'control', or 'not democratic', or we don't want the church full of 'yes men' –while all the time our greater problem is that too many are 'no men'. So in our hearts we assume this to be simply an ideal, with no greater purpose than to point us in the right direction, as far as humanly possible in our circumstances. And in the meantime, life is 'real' so we just get on with it, and relegate this verse to nothing more than an exhortation to better behaviour. Consequently, we see no fulfillment of it in *power*.

Paul goes on: *"...that there may be no divisions among you."* Not only has Paul said that all should agree, but that this would provide for a church without divisions among the people.

This he follows with a summary; *"...that you may be perfectly united in mind and thought."* Paul did not say 'united'; he said '*perfectly united*'.

Jesus said the Word of God cannot be broken, and the Word of God this remains. In the heart of God there is not only a desire that we live this way, but also a readiness to give a special grace that would enable us to do so. And we need such a special grace, because it is not possible to live perfectly united in mind and thought, to be of one accord, and to work together without division, out of human ability. But it certainly is possible when we find the divine grace, that special endowment, that has been made available for the purpose.

It would be helpful to relate the story of what happened to us – this you will find in the following chapters – of how things got worse before they got better, and how we finally found a power answer to our need.

CHAPTER-TWO

An Early *Revelation*

A Grace Called Understanding

"...and much grace was upon them all."

Acts 4: 33

At the time we had a huge problem. Our church was going through terrible division. I suppose it was, indirectly, very much over 'the apostolic', in so far as the Lord wanted to take our church on a whole new approach to international mission and some people just couldn't accept it. Through the deception and lies of only one or two, we ended up with enemies who worked hard against us, and caused a lot of division in a fellowship that had been without division. I had an inkling it was coming, for the Lord told me the year before, "Storm clouds are gathering." I knew what that meant. I sought the Lord and He said, "Let me do what I have to do with your people."

We managed to pray and trust our way through it the best way we could, falsely accused and despised by growing numbers. We were up for hours every night praying, and forgiving all the while. I always maintain there can be no room for bitterness, feeling sorry for ourselves, or living with regret – these things are not the way of Christ. We received the benefit of the trials and tribulation, for in the end, the great majority of the church was found standing with me, and those who remained the Lord then took on a remarkable journey.

In the middle of this – it was June 1998, and matters were coming to a head – I spent a month in prayer. I rested on the weekends, but on week days I was up at 4.30 a.m. to be at the church by 6.00 a.m., and there I would remain in prayer, usually on the floor down the front of the auditorium, until 6.00 p.m. I had announced to the church that anybody could join me at anytime, and various ones would come and go throughout the days. We were at that time experiencing the worst division, rancour, false accusation of leaders, and hatred that we had ever known in church life.

After many days, on about the 23rd of the month, at 6.15 a.m. while it was still dark and cold outside, I felt drawn to Psalm 32. I opened my Bible and read the Psalm. Verse 9 says, "*Do not be like the horse or the mule, which have no understanding but must be controlled by bit and bridle or they will not come to you.*" As I sat wondering why God was speaking to me about horses and mules, suddenly and instantaneously I received an amazing download of information, all based on that word *"understanding"*. It comprised both words and pictures, and fully formed concepts. In just a few moments I was flooded with knowledge of something God was saying, and these were things I could see and feel deeply.

Here is what the Lord gave me:

> He said He was looking for *a people*, in fact searching the earth to find a people, upon whom He could place *Understanding*. The size of the group, He said, didn't matter. It wouldn't matter whether it was 50 people or 200. What He was looking for was a group that would *allow* Him to place understanding upon them.
>
> He then stated that if He could find such a group that would allow Him to place this understanding upon them, it would totally transform their life as a people. They would become a people of one heart and one mind, they would rise as one man, and they would do the work of God in the world.
>
> I saw clearly that such a group that had upon them this spirit of understanding would have the kind of power that would profoundly affect the world and change nations – and nothing would be able to resist the grace they had been given, or hinder them from doing the will of God.

Once this experience was over, I found myself sitting there, Psalm 32 still open on my knee, and wondering. I started to question whether that was really God, or just me. Was it just me being idealistic? It seemed strange to me that God could just change a people like that. In my entire life I had never seen a group of Christians anywhere of whom it could be said they were of one heart and one mind. I asked myself, could this really be possible? Would we ever see this kind of thing this side of heaven?

I decided, if I was to believe that God could or would do this, there must be something in the Bible to confirm it. I quickly searched through the Scriptures and to my surprise found two actual examples of God doing this very thing. I was amazed – there was an example in the Old Testament, and another in the New. Every truth is established in the mouth of two or three witnesses.

For the Old Testament witness, 2 Chronicles 30:12 records: "…in Judah *the hand of God was on the people to give them unity of mind to carry out what the king and his officials had ordered, following the word of the Lord."* The recorded history of Israel is quite explicit; this kind of thing is just not an everyday event. But at least on this one occasion, God sovereignly acted to grant grace to His people for a purpose. And the witness is, God can and does, when He chooses, grant grace to work unity of heart, mind, and purpose in the lives of His people.

Then coming to the New Testament I 'found' the witness of Acts 4:32, *"All the believers were one in heart and mind."* And verse 33 adds, *"…and much grace was upon them all."* When I read those words I was convinced, God had indeed spoken and revealed His purpose.

The state of the church as described in Acts 4:32 was the result of what God did, both leading up to and at *Pentecost.* He had specially prepared that group of people, so that when He poured out His Spirit it produced an outcome which, years later, Luke could truthfully record, *"All the believers were one in heart and mind."*

It is a truly amazing statement to say that all the people were of one heart and one mind. *All* is a very 'large' number in that it leaves no exceptions, especially when we take into consideration that thousands of people were coming to the faith, including many Jewish priests. Obviously then, this is a state of grace, not normal to human nature. Neither does the fact that it was a church make this state normal. We have all belonged to churches that were not of one heart and one mind, even though we all believe the things these early Christians believed. We will come to understand why as we proceed through this book.

Being born again does not in itself automatically cause believers to be of one heart and mind with other believers. That ought to be obvious since we have churches everywhere comprised of many born-again believers demonstrating that this alone does not cause astounding unity. Something more, then, is needed. What is this grace, and how do we obtain it? We see the first church clearly enjoying this grace. How is it, then, that we have lost it?

Do you remember what the Lord said He was doing? Searching the earth for a people who would *allow* Him to place on them what He called understanding. You would think that just about any church would want this. What then does it mean to *allow*?

Every one of us would tell the Lord we were willing, so obviously the notion of allowing God to do this goes beyond saying 'Yes please'. God is not just thinking of our requesting it when He says He is looking for a willing people.

There must be something more to this 'allowing' God. Note too that what He is looking to find is something in the heart of a *people*, not just in the heart of an individual. It must involve God so working with a group over time that they come to a place where something within them enables God to give this to them. Perhaps it takes years of preparing them, conditioning them, training, disciplining, and sifting them. There must be something in them that has changed, something broken, something yielded, that relates to their willingness to receive such a grace.

And further, they must be willing to accept the outcomes from that grace at work, along with whatever price is to be paid in suffering and sacrifice as a result of being so yielded, and therefore sent. To be willing to receive the grace also means being willing to receive the consequences that come from it. For that to be the case, God first has to prepare the hearts of the people, because this great grace will come with great responsibility.

Yes, I began to pray for this grace. The Lord had not said He was looking at us, or considering our church; He simply said He was looking throughout the world to find even one group. I did preach about this to our church, and we prayed through it, but nothing seemed to happen. As I travelled I preached it in other places too, simply because I wanted to build the faith of others, and hold out a vision and hope to pastors and their people, offering something of great value for which to hunger in Christ.

But as one year turned into another, the vision became overlooked and forgotten in the detail of a busy life in the ministry.

CHAPTER-THREE

SEARCHING FOR 'Community'

"Ask and it will be given to you;
seek and you will find;
knock and the door will be opened to you."
Luke 11: 9

In January, 1988, I took over the leadership of a Baptist church in North Rockhampton. They had asked if I would lead them into renewal, and this presented an exciting challenge. The church was full of very good-hearted believers who were hungry for God. They responded so positively to what was taught, and the Holy Spirit helped us greatly as many people came into the baptism of the

Spirit. We discovered Biblical gifts and graces. Healing in particular became a powerful ministry amongst us, and freedom in worship became established. There was great joy in our hearts.

The Journey of Peace

Although this was a Baptist church, we didn't keep the Baptist 'label' for very long; but neither did we take on any other labels. Yes, we enjoyed discovering the charismatic/ Pentecostal dimension of Christian experience, but I somehow knew the Lord was doing something completely new which should not be limited by labeling it Pentecostal. That was fine for an era, but I felt sure He was moving the whole church on to something better, something greater; something that was even more fully and truly Christ, if that were possible. We did not understand then, but realised some time later, that God was restoring the apostolic nature of His people, and the whole church was being led to find what it means to share an apostolic *life*.

Our church was growing too, and people from other denominational backgrounds were joining us. There were Lutheran, Anglican, Uniting Church, Salvation Army, and Pentecostal people, as well as others. I used to say to the church, "God is doing something completely new. Don't bring preconceived ideas and traditions in with you. Come in and be willing to sit, listen to the Lord, and wait. These things are not done in five minutes. There is a process going on, and we need to be prepared for the Lord to make something fresh and new of us."

Of all the people coming in, it was the Pentecostals who needed most to hear that word, and to try and put assumptions aside. The reason for this was that they tended to be more convinced of their own spirituality, and confident of their ability to operate in spiritual gifts – and they had come from church cultures where it was believed without question, and perhaps not without reason, that they were more in the Spirit than other churches, with, they thought, a better corporate worship and prayer life. So, some tended to think, with their words of knowledge and prophecy and all, how could they not be in the centre of the will of God?

They were good people, but thought they had to urge the rest of us to go where they thought they were. But we were not meant to stay focused on where they had been, as good as that might have been, for God was taking the church where none of us, including them, had ever been.

The Quest for Community

Our stated goal had been to find the secret of community. For years we taught on this theme, seeking to bring our people into an experience of deeper relationships. We taught often on the need for intimacy and faithfulness in relationships, of a covenant understanding of our relationships in Christ, of serving one another, of being open and transparent and devoted to one another.

We formed cells, thinking that as they prayed and shared with one another in small groups their hearts would be knit more closely. We studied cell structure, went to cell conferences, and instituted cell procedures, in pursuit of our goal of building community. This still did not bring the desired experience of community, and though we re-organised the cells in various ways, we could not seem to make them fruitful as we wanted. For seven years we continued teaching cell life and community values, but still felt we were no closer to our goal, for the things taught did not of themselves seem to produce community in the hearts of the people.

Seeking to Build Community

To all intents and purposes ours was a sound and genuine church. But somehow deep down in our hearts, David Hood and I, amongst others, knew that this was not yet what God wanted for us. We would often sit at my desk, me on one side and he on the other, and ponder together the mystery. We knew by our training and background how to build an institutional church, an organisational form of Christianity, but we had never been taught how to build a church on relationships.

Anyone could gather people and say they have a church. But unless there is some dynamic that has knit those people together into oneness, is it really a church? And we used to discuss how to move from program to community. How do we stop building institutionally and start building relationally? This for us was the big question of church life.

It was not as if the church was not doing well in other ways. No, in truth there were great things happening all the time, with powerful manifestations of the Holy Spirit, converts and baptisms, and a good mission programme. Our worship services were wonderful, the people were generous givers, and we had great nights of prayer. We saw wonderful healings and answers to prayer. We would stand as one on Sunday mornings and pray united prayer for people in various parts of the world, who were often instantly healed of very serious conditions. We had a great property too, on twenty-five acres in town with many facilities. Any observer would say we had a wonderful church, with good people serving Christ. But it was not yet exactly what we were looking for.

And it's not that we didn't have a basic, decent unity – we had a co-operative, worshipping, generous, prayerful, and hard-working people – but admittedly, looking back, all that was mixed in with too much prideful independence and hidden denominational assumptions in 'Christian' mindsets. We didn't understand the difference, but knew enough to be looking for something deeper in terms of intimacy of relationship. We had a Bible College, a High School and Primary School. There was money flowing in, we sent teams overseas –the point I am making is that outwardly we had what one usually judges by to say a church is effective.

One night in prayer, walking around the church building, I heard the Lord say, *"I am going to bring you into a deep unity of the Spirit. When your teams go out they will minister with great power, but the power will come because of the unity at home."* I thought we had a great unity already and the Lord was simply going to improve on it. I hadn't heard that theory of community which says we start with pseudo-community, then go through chaos to find true community.

We had enjoyed good times from 1988 through to 1996, with the church growing and an atmosphere of progress. It all felt good. Thus I did not realise that when the Lord said He was going to bring us into a deep unity of the Spirit, this meant we were in for trouble.

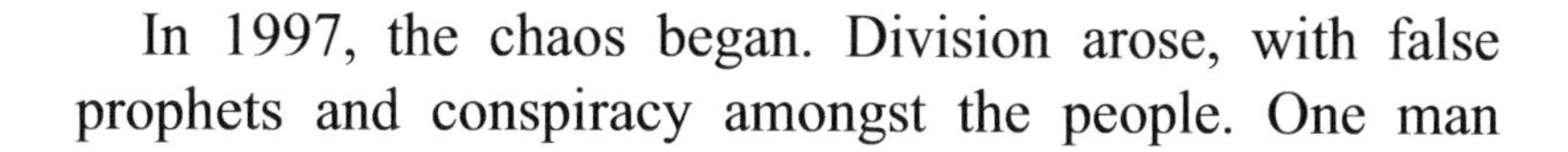

In 1997, the chaos began. Division arose, with false prophets and conspiracy amongst the people. One man set his heart on destroying me and the church. You could not imagine the manifestation of Satan that rose in a few of those people, even some who had been very close to me. Irrationally, friends became bitter enemies overnight, believing things that were never true, and you couldn't reason with them. How did the devil get in?

In retrospect, it was the Lord who put us through the chaos which shook the church. At the time we knew that to be true, but it was still very difficult nevertheless. We lost numbers of people over a period of eighteen months or so. At the end of it, more than two-thirds of our people remained, standing with me through it all, loving and believing.

I have a friend who is the pastor of a wonderful church that went through similar turmoil last year. Recently I wrote and offered him the following encouragement:

> *"I have been reflecting on our history, since I am writing a new book on community, and realise now, more than ever, that our troubles, and people vilifying us and leaving, was a very important part of a process that positioned us for the breakthroughs in church life we have had. Not that we ever want the chaos, but it is amazing how much we can find God in the midst, very present and working powerfully in lives at such times."*

When our period of opposition was over, we found it so quiet, so stable, and so peaceful in the church. However, this we found was just the beginning of a second period of refining – that of insignificance and powerlessness – in which our hearts and sense of identity were tested in other ways. I have spoken of this in an earlier book. But this period was very fruitful, because the leaders of the ministry began to spend a lot of time together – not in church business meetings, but in personal conversation, in homes, and in days of prayer. The outcome was close personal relationships, trust, and a growing transparency. We had become friends, but more. We were being glued together by a work of grace. Love between us was real, and personal. And the most important meetings we held were not held for any formal reason.

This was a really important process leading towards the relational life we wanted for the church, and it led to the following event.

The Public Testimony of Peace Leaders

There was a Sunday morning, somewhere in the year 2000, when we dispensed with the usual preaching and instead I stood up with my wife Hazel, and with my associate pastors David and Judy, and Tony and Carolyn. Between the six of us we took over an hour to tell our people how we felt about each other, and how we felt about them. We talked about the kind of love that was in our hearts for one another, and the genuine love we felt for that congregation. I told them honestly that I had other offers and opportunities, but though I had been treated badly by some who had now left, very badly by some who had tried to destroy the church, and though I had felt constrained from speaking in my own defence over the two years of opposition, nevertheless I remained as leader because I loved them.

It would have been easy to leave, and a lot of pastors do. Who can blame them, and some have no choice. As for me, I have come into a huge inheritance because I stayed right there.

I was willing to lay it down. I didn't grasp it, I wasn't clinging to it. My wife and I were on our faces before God for long hours saying, "Lord, you can take everything away from us if you wish. You can take the ministry. You can take our home, you can take our property. Whatever you want to take, you can have it all. Just let us know the will of God." He made it really clear that we should stay, so we stayed. But deep down, I felt another reason – and a year or two later I told the church there was another reason I stayed. I could not get away from the love that so many had for me. And I had promised I would provide the leadership they wanted, so that together we might find our way to the 'mountain of God', and my heart was for them.

Recently, on a long Qantas flight, when the plane was dark and everyone resting, I made my way to the galley to get a decent cup of tea. I got into conversation with a steward who asked what I did. After I briefly explained my mission, he asked why I didn't operate out of a big city. What, with ministry all over the world, and needing support and seeking to build a strong work, he wanted to know why I didn't go and base myself in Sydney or Brisbane. It would be easy to do that, but I am not going anywhere. The answer I gave him was that I had good people to whom I was committed, and they were committed to me. I had given my heart to those people, and had no desire to leave them to find others who might offer me more.

Autumn Rain

In March 2002, we held the first of our now annual Autumn Rain Camps. I felt an unusual leading, and I told my senior associate, David, that we were to prepare no messages and make very little worship preparation for the meetings. I told the worship leader, Carolyn, to take fewer songs than she thought we would need. Further, I said, I will just sit in the front row, and say nothing in any meeting unless the Holy Spirit gives me something specific to say. I asked David to provide the leadership to guide the meetings through.

I had no idea what David would do, with so little to work with. When I arrived, I found he had placed all the chairs in a circle, or rather, three circles, one inside the other. Even the worship leader, musicians and singers were part of the circle. At the commencement of the first meeting, he simply asked people to begin the weekend by sharing their expectations of what God would do over the weekend. Then he put the microphone on the table, and sat down.

First one, then another, and then a third person came to the microphone and gave testimonies of glowing expectations. But when the third person put the microphone down and began to move away, she froze in a trance next to the table, and stayed in that exact place for the next two and a half hours.

One by one more people came, but their testimonies began to change, beginning to speak not so much of their expectations of the camp, but of their hopes and fears in life, and what they were looking to God to do. They spoke of the way they felt about things, and specifically the way they felt about each other. This went on for a long time until, after about an hour and a half, David felt we should sing a song. When we began to sing, it was like heaven came down, and we moved on to a second song and a third. Then the Spirit of God lifted right off the worship, so we stopped the song and went back to sharing. The sharing went on for another long period, with our sister still frozen in the midst of it all.

Throughout the meeting I sat saying nothing, but something was really going on in the hearts of the people. There had been no prayers, no preaching, very little singing, but it was the most powerful and sovereignly-led Holy Spirit meeting, and series of meetings, I have seen amongst our people, and led in turn to wonderful things that followed.

Those experiences at Family Camp were part of a long series of breakthroughs and events in which God was dealing with us, and which led to the teaching in my previous two books, and this one. These times changed the way we walk with each other, 'see' each other, and feel about each other. In other words, it changed the church from the inside out. When we speak of changing the church, we do not mean external things, such as structures, so much as God wanting to change the hearts of His people. It is the way we 'operate', the way we think and feel about each other, that has to change.

In the process we came to an understanding of fathering and sonship relationships in the ministry of Jesus Christ. I came to the place where I really connected with apostle Chuck Clayton, who had been my apostolic covering and spiritual father in theory for eight years. It was at this time that I discovered what it felt like to be a son from the heart. I felt like I had a father. It felt like we belonged - that he belonged to us and we belonged to him. It was a phenomenal shift in our hearts and in the whole church too for that matter. We had breakthroughs in many lives with respect to that spiritual truth becoming experience by the grace of God. And once we got this breakthrough on the fathering and sonship issue, wherein it became experiential and emotive, i.e. of the heart, and not just systemic and organisational, within a few months I had a dream.

The Dream: There is an Anointing

I had the dream one night late in September, 2002, and when I woke, felt compelled to seek the Lord to understand its meaning. I sat with the Lord, and He said something I was not expecting, and had no inkling of. The word He gave me was to change everything, as you will see.

CHAPTER-FOUR

THE KEY: AN *Anointing* FOR BUILDING COMMUNITY

"By the grace God has given me,
I laid a foundation as an expert builder,
and someone else is building on it.
But each one should be careful how he builds."
1 Corinthians 3: 10

By September, 2002, a greater apostolic anointing was being released over the Body of Christ, although we didn't really see it at the time. Waiting on God for the meaning of the dream, He said:

"There is an anointing by which community is built."

"Oh," I thought, "that means we don't have it."

Nothing could have been more obvious to me – if we had tried persistently, as we had, to build community, but without results, and if at the same time there exists an anointing for building community, it can only mean one thing – we did not have that anointing!

Then He said:

"And there is another anointing by which leaders perceive community."

"Oh," I thought, "we don't have that one either."

An Anointing is Grace, and Grace is Power

Now I felt I was on to something. *There is an anointing.* If there is an anointing, that means there is a *grace*. And a grace, when received, is power. A lot of people do not put it in these terms, but grace is not just God's feeling about us. Many stop there because they define grace as God's mercy. Grace is much more than mercy. Let me tell you that whenever grace is received, power is always received.

Can we prove that? What about when someone is born again by the Spirit? Is it God just feeling good about them and blotting out their sins? No, you know that the transformation of life is so real, so permanent, so definite – this person previously hated righteousness and loved wickedness, but now loves righteousness and hates wickedness. That takes power. When grace is given, power is always received.

I need to mention that by the time of this dream, I was no longer thinking about the earlier revelation I described in Chapter 2, so did not apply what He had shown me at that time to our current situation. But this new word came as a solution to an immediate need, and it held hope and wonderment for me. *"There is an anointing,"* He had said, *"by which community is built."* These were exciting words to me, as was His second statement: *"There is another anointing, by which leaders perceive community."* To perceive means to be able to apprehend, to have a heart for, and be able to look into, to longingly take hold of, to have a big heart to grasp it, and to have a vision to build it.

As I pondered this anointing by which community is built, it occurred to me that I had never noticed this in the Bible. I had seen all kinds of other anointings there, such as the power to heal the sick, and the grace given for some to be apostles or pastors. But the idea of *this* being an anointing I had not seen anywhere in Scripture, I thought. However, if it was true, and if I was to believe what I had heard, then it had to be found in the Bible.

When I went in search of that anointing, it didn't take long to find Pentecost all over again – and find it with new eyes. When God poured out the Holy Spirit, he poured out many anointings – in fact, in the coming of the Holy Spirit, He came with every grace and gift that are in Christ – and these are all available. There was anointing for tongues and healing and prophecy and walking with God and guidance and all. But the central anointing, the core anointing, around which all these other things are attached, is the anointing by which all the believers became a people – which is why they became of one heart and one mind. Once we realise this, we see the bigger picture of Pentecost. Pentecost always had as its primary purpose the forming of holy community.

And with this light, I discovered my eyes were open to see, from Acts 2 through to Acts 12 and beyond, the community anointing clearly at work among the people. Much of the way the church operated in the Acts of the Apostles could only be because of that anointing.

For example, in Chapter 12 it is recorded that the apostle James was arrested and Herod put him to death by the sword. Herod then arrested Peter and was going to kill him too. Then this telling line is written; "but the church was earnestly praying to God for him."

They had not offered much prayer for James. Presumably there was an assumption that apostles would be OK, for they had been arrested before. But in fact, the church must pray: even apostles are not necessarily safe if the church does not pray for them. The church needs apostles, and apostles also need the church.

And when the church offered much prayer for Peter, there occurred a tremendous series of miracles. Peter's chains fell off, the angel had to wake him up, and even though he was chained to soldiers, they did not notice the chains fall off him. They did not even see Peter getting up and walking to the door, which opened of its own accord. He then walked past more guards, who were all wide awake, but saw nothing. In front of him were the big prison gates, with more guards. Again, the gates opened and the guards saw nothing. Is this a series of many miracles, or just one event? Where did the church get such power? From the account, it came from a prayer meeting in a house.

I have been in many prayer meetings where we have offered much prayer, and received answers to prayer too. We've all seen miracles, but not the likes of that one. There is a reason why those people saw, I believe, that kind of miracle; they were in community. They were of one heart and one mind, and when that grace is present, the church has much more power.

Now we at Peace were not without anointings. We had many anointings – for worship, for finance, for healing, for teaching, for mission, for leadership, for prayer, for pastoral care, for preaching the gospel, and so on. But we did *not* have what was described to me as "the anointing by which community is built." That one was missing.

In defense against this argument that you also might not have this anointing, you might point to signs of love. You can say, "We have got people who love each other," and of course you do. We had people who loved each other too. We had lots of them. They were people who loved the Lord, and would worship and pray. Intercession was very strong with us. We had all these things, but still there was something more that was needed.

Could I say it is probably the same with most churches: God is with them, there is a lot of blessing, but there is still a missing anointing.

And God was with us. We were still seeing people saved, and the power of the Holy Spirit would come into our meetings and move upon the people. Sometimes people would fall off their chairs drunk with the Holy Spirit, others would be glued to the floor under the power of the Holy Spirit, being dealt with by a gracious God. The Holy Spirit was at work, and yet there was something we still did not have the power to do.

But now that I had this word from the Lord, I knew what I needed to do; it was simple enough. And I have discovered that if there is any need or any lack, what we then must find is an impartation of grace into that area. For everything that we are called to do, there is an anointing.

The following Sunday morning I preached about what the Lord had said, and showed the church the things I had found in Acts 2-12. Then I prayed over the congregation, and with a simple prayer, by faith brought that anointing down from the throne of grace, and released it into the hearts of the believers. This is a straightforward work of grace in leadership authority, and I was very fortunate that over the previous ten years I had learned how to receive anointings and how to release anointings in ministry. I had also learned that in a meeting there is always a group anointing present, and it is possible to release an anointing to a whole group of people in an instant. And because I had that experience, I also had faith, which put me in a good position for what needed to be done. And thus I prayed, although there was no immediate effect to be seen – and I wasn't necessarily expecting one. The service closed, we had coffee, and all went home. The next Sunday there was nothing different to see, nor the next week nor the next.

But after six weeks, at the weekly leaders' fellowship at my house, one of the pastors on the staff, Tony, came in with a story. He dropped into a lounge chair, and very casually remarked that for many years he had tried his best, in every way he knew, to get our cells to work, but no matter what he did, he could not seem to make them work. So he gave up trying. "But a very strange thing has happened," he remarked. "About six weeks ago, all those cells started working all on their own." The mention of six weeks caused me to sit up and take notice; I knew it had been six weeks since I had released that anointing. He said the cells had started working *all on their own*. This meant that grace, 'the anointing by which community is built,' was at work in the hearts of the people.

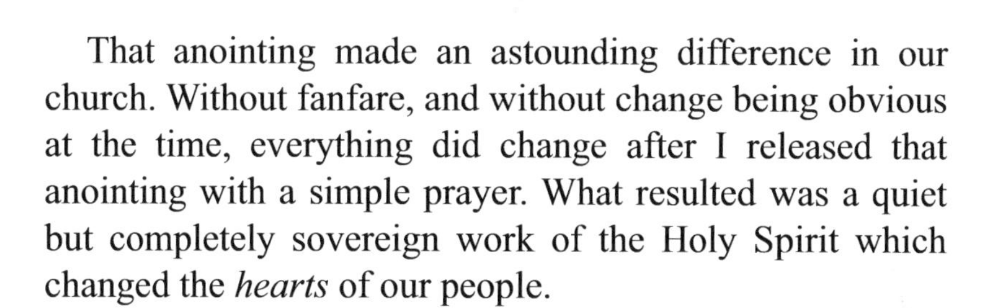

That anointing made an astounding difference in our church. Without fanfare, and without change being obvious at the time, everything did change after I released that anointing with a simple prayer. What resulted was a quiet but completely sovereign work of the Holy Spirit which changed the *hearts* of our people.

Two primary things changed in our hearts. The first is that our people seemed to see each other with a different set of eyes. Of course, the truth is, they saw each other with a different heart.

One sister testified, sometime later, that there was another woman in the church that she couldn't stand, didn't want to sit anywhere near, and always felt rubbed up the wrong way by her. She found it very uncomfortable to be around her and used to avoid her. But she found her heart had completely changed. She no longer felt uncomfortable, but instead appreciated her very much. Since the time the grace was released, she felt great love, admiration, and acceptance of that person. It was a total change of feeling and outlook, with no human explanation.

This is what I mean by saying that our people now saw each other through different eyes.

The other wonderful change was that inter-personal striving was removed from church life, along with selfish agendas. There was no more competition, or people trying to get their own way. Talk about a peaceful life!

There were practical outcomes too. For one, people stopped leaving the church. Previously we would work hard to keep everybody together, yet even so from time to time people would leave for no good reason. We had had a series of unfortunate 'losses' even in the years after the nasty time of division was over and calm had returned. But from the time the community grace was received, virtually all abnormal movement out ceased.

Tony tells me (and it has now been almost eight years) that the amount of counseling or serious pastoral care required by our own people dropped to a fraction of what it was before.

As a people, we have come to the place where we simply belong to each other. The atmosphere within the church changed, and this has made a big difference to me. Up until that time I had needed to work hard as the pastor, but when that grace came in, I relaxed completely. Previously, I would set the alarm to get up extra early on Sunday morning to pray at length, before preparing carefully, dressing well, and arriving at the church early. I would make sure I said hello to everybody before the service started. I would work hard, and feel under pressure, to make sure we had a great programme, great worship, great announcements, great preaching and great ministry times, and then when finished I would go around and try to greet everybody again.

Why was it so important to operate like that? Because we had to keep our 'customers' happy. If we didn't keep them happy, they might go down the road and shop in another pastor's shopping centre. Much of the church is like this; striving, competitive, and performance-oriented.

But the coming of the grace for community changed all that. It made us feel that we belonged to each other. Something shifted in the hearts of the people, and things felt different because they *were* different. Now when I turn up on Sunday, I have come home. I walk into that building and I am with family who love me. I walk in and relax like the rest of the people. I belong, not just organisationally, but in their hearts. By the way people greet me it is obvious they feel they belong to me, and I belong to them. We have all come home. There is no more sense of threat or dread in the house. When I get up to speak, God begins to speak and there is no more need to 'perform', and no more spirit of competition. There is rest in the hearts of the people. And I don't even set the alarm anymore.

The church was good before, and the people were good people. But this was a remarkable miracle we received, and it took place in the heart of all the people as a whole at the same time. I am not saying that we don't have those who, as in all churches, dwell on the fringes of the church, and haven't fully received of this grace, but I am talking about the spirit of the whole. And I am not saying that it is a perfect work, or that the process is complete. We have yet to complete our journey together. And there will always be those who, whether newcomers, or those lukewarm who have never surrendered, are in a place where they still need to receive the word of God and let it transform them. Neither can the church be judged as deficient if occasionally some false brethren try to enter, or some independent ones attempt to come in with their own agendas – at least there will always be an opportunity to minister truth and correction to the unruly. But these do not really belong, although they have the opportunity to stay and be healed and find a home with us.

We are ordinary people, with our share of faults and weaknesses, but we are really happy in appreciating and giving grace to each other. We didn't fully realise how this works with us, until recently a couple with such an unruly spirit came to join us. Of course, these kind of folk are usually bright and cheerful on the outside, presenting as victorious Christians, and excited about how great is the church they've come to join. But within a matter of a few weeks they quickly became super critical and condemning of some of the families in the church.

I will spare you the tale of their background, but in visiting some of the families in the church for meals, and being welcomed amongst us with great love, they could only see fault in people. After a few short weeks, these people would openly criticise and condemn the family life of good people. Their views were harsh and judgmental in the extreme, and some of their claims were delusional. They spoke to us about families that they considered dysfunctional, and referred to various people as 'no good'. I had not seen such wickedness in people for a long time.

One Sunday morning I was sitting in church as they walked in, silhouetted in the doorway. I heard the Lord say, "The spirit of community is not in them." It was such a pity. They had read the books, heard the CDs, loved and agreed with the teaching – but did not have the grace.

We confronted them over their sin, and they left town as quickly as they had come. However, at the following Tuesday afternoon weekly leaders' relational meeting, I suggested that we not assume we had no fault, and that it would be best to see this as an opportunity to examine our own hearts. Was God allowing this for our good, and should we correct ourselves in some way? So around the dining table in our house we went to prayer to consider before God if there was any truth in their claims they made about us or our people.

My eldest son David was present, and spoke to the question with a greatly helpful insight. He said something to this effect: "The reason the people of Peace love each other so much, and there is such grace in the house, is because they do not have expectations of each other. If there is no expectation of performance, then there will be no criticism and condemnation when people do not perform."

To have expectations of a person is to expect some kind of outward conformity, but when expectations are not present, we are free to love the person for who they are. Without realising it, this was a big part of our secret. Human beings cannot change themselves. When a person is born again, they do not change themselves. Neither do they change themselves when they receive the baptism in the Holy Spirit.

I thank God for what we have received at Peace, but I know there's more. There is a still greater measure of this grace available. I know that on the day I released the anointing by which community is built, it changed our people forever. In particular, striving and disjointedness were removed. But I do hasten to add, I have never believed we have yet obtained all of this particular grace. I often remark at home that we received a down payment, and we are to look for a larger portion. Nevertheless, it markedly changed the hearts of our people and brought in greater oneness and the bonds of love. Since then, our whole church has been redefined, and we now send teams all over Australia and the world, something we never did before.

I perceive that this anointing by which community is built is probably the same grace that the Lord referred to in speaking with me in 1998 as the spirit of understanding, which was one of the seven primary anointings resting upon the Lord Jesus Christ. We shall yet discuss this further.

We have come to the place where we simply belong to each other. We have made some progress in the journey to find community, and it has a great deal to do with how we feel about each other; we belong.

And if we have nothing else to offer the body of Christ, we do have this: that we love each other.

May I, at this point, draw two conclusions?

One Mind – the Intended Normal State of the Church

In considering the Pentecost story and its outcomes, along with all the things the apostle Paul in particular had to say about hearts and minds in the churches, what seems evident to me is that this state of blessing and anointing – the one-heart one-mind state – was meant to be the normal state of the church. Not a one-off thing, nor an occasional thing, but rather, this was how the church was birthed, and how we can remain.

Whilst this was meant to be the kind of life the church shares, what we've too often known is a striving, competitive kind of church life – with all the usual problems such as ambition, selfishness, backbiting, and the like, taking their toll. I can in all honesty say with regard to the latter, that at home we haven't seen this kind of thing as part of corporate church life in years. It is an entirely different culture we enjoy. The Lord really did change our people, and what I am speaking of is real. There is a grace available, and it is worth finding this anointing.

The Power we see in the Book of Acts came from Community

After the account of the pouring out of the Holy Spirit in Acts Chapter 2, there are recorded constant and regular indicators of things happening in the early Church that could only happen to a people in community. That is, the level of power and authority that we see evidenced there, and the amount and kind of signs and wonders, miracles, and answers to prayer they enjoyed, were outcomes of the Church being in community. This is a major difference between Christianity as we usually know it and the apostolic Church as it then was.

Externally, we look at it and see they had great power, while we don't seem to have much power ourselves. The text of Acts 4 says that with great power the apostles bore witness to the resurrection, and there were many signs and wonders, and much grace was upon them. That does not sound a lot like any congregation that most of us have been a part of. We wonder where this apostolic power has gone, and long for the days of apostolic grace again.

Throughout the years I have often heard preaching about the need for apostolic power to be restored to the Church.

But we were missing the fact that this level of grace and power flows from, or through, community. Generally, the kind of institutional Christianity we have known has not had this depth of relationship in it. But when the Spirit of God was given on the day of Pentecost, and the hearts of the people were knit together, it created a community through which the power of the Spirit could flow with great effect.

CHAPTER-FIVE

A MUTUAL ADMIRATION *Society*

"Be devoted to one another in brotherly love.
Honour one another above yourselves."
Romans 12: 10

In chapter two I described the word given to me in 1998 revealing God's heart to find a people upon whom He could place *understanding,* a grace which totally transforms the shared life of the group and makes them so powerful and fruitful in sacrificial service to Christ. You will remember that I presented two Biblical examples which served as witnesses to this truth, the second being the day of Pentecost

– which is more than a witness; it is in itself a revelation of God's grace and purpose. Now I want you to consider a third witness – for afterwards the Lord gave me one more example, this time from church history. It is found in the well-known story of Count Zinzendorf and the group of believers known as the Moravian Brethren.

An Example found in Church History

The Moravians, which is how they are usually referred to, had a 330 year history, over which period they had quite some wonderful Christian leaders and teachers. But, at the time of our story, they had become refugees – Christian refugees – fleeing persecution, and ending up in Germany, where they linked with a great Christian man, a wealthy German prince, Count Zinzendorf. Zinzendorf is often referred to as 'the rich young ruler who said "Yes" to Jesus.'

Count Zinzendorf had vast land holdings, and the refugees asked if they could settle on his estate and build a town in which to live. Zinzendorf and his wife were both devoted servants of Christ, and he allowed the refugees to build their town, called Herrnhut, which means, "the Lord's watch" or "the watch of the Lord." Zinzendorf became their pastor.

This little church had all the problems that churches everywhere have to deal with in the lives of their people. They had their struggles and every kind of human relationship issue that you have seen in churches anywhere. There occurred jealousy and envy, backbiting and competition, striving with one another, and as well, the usual gossip and selfish ambition. They had a false prophet arise who tried to lead the people astray. And there was a split, and rebellion, where some of them wanted to get rid of Zinzendorf. Basically, they experienced every kind of fleshly weakness and evil striving that comes up from time to time in the experience of churches all over the world. Though they had a great Christian history, and though they were related to one another, in many ways they were a 'mixed multitude' too, as was Israel when it came out of Egypt.

They had a very good Christian 'pedigree'. They could trace their spiritual heritage back over three hundred years to Peter Cominos, a great teacher, and the famous martyr John Huss, a great pioneer for the Reformation who was burned at the stake before the time of Luther. But such a lineage, and the fact that they knew each other well, and had been together a long time, did not mean their spiritual life at the time they founded Herrnhut was any better than many churches today.

Most reading this will have a good 'pedigree' too. You are in good churches, with good pastors. You've had good doctrine, and good experiences of God, and your faith is well-established, but despite that there is still in many a struggle with striving, jealousies, ambition, resentment of the success of others, and so on. The Moravians in Herrnhut had been no different, and all of their Christian history was not able to keep them from it.

Zinzendorf was a godly man, and spent much time in prayer. One night, with trouble on his hands, he spent the whole night crying out to God in prayer for the church. Heaven heard, and soon after that, on Sunday, August 13th, 1727, something happened that in Church history is known as the Moravian Pentecost.

That Sunday morning they were sharing a communion service when the Holy Spirit quietly moved in their hearts. Unlike the Day of Pentecost, there was nothing to see or hear. There were no tongues of fire or other outward signs. But the Holy Spirit, sovereignly bringing a great grace into the hearts of the people, totally and completely changed them for good.

One of their number, in recording their history, preserved two vital pieces of information that help us understand what happened that morning. The historian said, *"It seemed as if God had taken all our differences out of our hearts,"* and he further said, *"We became a people who greatly admired each other."*

These two things we need to note. They are defining statements, and let us be very clear: these statements will be true of every church that finds the same grace that was given to the Moravians on that day.

The first statement was: it seemed as if all our differences were removed from our hearts. The word 'differences' is a common expression in the English language in reference to our disagreements, squabbles, struggles, striving with one another, jealousies, backbiting, division, etc. It is when we try to pull in two different directions. They said it seemed that God had removed all these from their hearts.

The other statement of the historian was: they became a people who greatly admired each other. And that leads us to a great definition for what each local church is meant to be – a mutual admiration society.

When you find this grace, which I have indicated is a Pentecostal grace, you will find that the Holy Spirit will have done in your people these two things. He will have removed from the hearts of your people the spirit of striving and competition, and He will have caused them to have a different way of seeing each other.

Regarding the accomplishments of the Moravians as a result of this grace becoming theirs, Church history tells us that this small group of people did more to evangelise the entire world in the following twenty years, than the entire Church of the whole world had done in the previous 200 years. They commenced a prayer meeting that ran 24 hours a day, without ceasing for 114 years. They sent their missionaries especially to the most difficult parts of the world, and many of them were martyred. At one stage, for every new missionary they sent out, one was somewhere being martyred. They came to the place where one family would stay at home and work hard to support two families in the field. Two young men amongst them heard of 3000 slaves living on an island to which no minister or Christian missionary was ever allowed, for the plantation owner hated Christianity. Those two young men sold themselves into slavery for life, so they could get onto that island and give their lives to win those slaves for Christ. As they boarded ship and were farewelling their parents and loved ones from the church, never to see them again, they were asked their reason for doing this. They said it was so Christ could have the inheritance for which He died. From the day of the Moravian Pentecost to the death of Zinzendorf 27 years later, the Moravians sent out of that small group some 250 missionaries across the world.

John Wesley said the like of their faith and fearless Christianity he had never seen anywhere, and there was nothing like it in all of England. It was seeing some of these Moravians that caused him to become so hungry to find God that Wesley was converted, and most of us today are spiritual children of Wesley in one way or another. We have to thank God for the grace He gave the Moravian Brethren.

That little group was no bigger than your church or mine, or perhaps as big as two or three of our churches together. We have all received the Holy Spirit, and we ought to ask why we are not like those people. The answer is, God gave those Moravians something that formed community in them, whereas most church fellowships are merely a group of individuals. Something in the way we relate to one another and walk with one another must change if we want to see the power of God.

The Moravians are a precise picture of everything the Lord said He could do with a people, and was now looking to do again according to that revelation concerning understanding. Their shared life was totally transformed, they became one in heart and mind, they rose as one to do the work of God in the world, nothing could resist or hinder the grace that was in them, and they powerfully changed their world.

Two Direct Outcomes of the Anointing

When a proper portion of this grace comes upon a church fellowship as a whole, hearts are changed and a new 'culture', one more consistently in keeping with love, apostolic life, and the New Testament exhortations, is established. And with this, there are two things that seem always to happen simultaneously. In fact, these two powerful changes are what define the work of this anointing, since they are the foundation for, or component parts of, the 'one heart – one mind' state of grace.

Remember, though, this anointing does not have to come in a dramatically obvious way as it did at Pentecost – it is just as well established by the Holy Spirit moving quietly in hearts, as He did with the Moravians, or as in our case, not even noticeable on the day. But remember also, we are talking about a group effect, an anointing coming upon believers as a body, which produces the following fruit:

1. Removal of the Spirit of Competition

Frankly, some kind of displacement takes place. Something is quite specifically taken out of the heart at the same time that something else is put in. The thing taken out of the heart I refer to as the *spirit of competition*, which is that part of human nature that causes us to strive with one another. This is the tendency to selfish ambition, to feel jealous, to resent others, to be independent, to want our own way and to rise above others, the desire to be thought of highly by others, or be considered successful in the eyes of others, or simply to want more success in life than others. This is common to us all, including children in the playground. We are all born with some kind of striving in us, as surely as Jacob was born grasping Esau's heel.

Here is what it is often like, with believers, in churches. We want to be noticed. We want our opinion accepted, and we want our prophecies honoured. We desire advancement, and are disappointed when someone else is chosen instead of us. Often there is not a lot of care whether someone else succeeds or not, but *we* want to succeed. It is in the human heart to take offense, to be envious, to believe we are better than or at least as good as others, and so on. All this we can summarise as the spirit of competition – it is just old-fashioned independence, pride, contention, striving with others, superiority, impatience, jealousy, resentment, the need to get ahead or look better than others, and so on.

Furthermore it is evident that this spirit of competition is not necessarily removed from our hearts when we are born again, because there are churches everywhere full of believers who are born again, but still striving. Many are the strong, evangelical, Bible-teaching churches with large numbers of truly born-again believers that still struggle daily with the issues of competition in the fellowship.

Neither is the spirit of competition necessarily removed when believers are baptised with the Holy Spirit, for similarly do we have large numbers of Pentecostal churches all over the world that have to deal with this competition in the fellowship as a 'normal' part of church life. We have churches with powerful ministries and empowered believers which still struggle with selfish ambition and control at work. A 'performance' orientation is very common here too, perhaps even more so, since there is an emphasis on everyone exercising their spiritual gifts. In a culture of 'success', where an independent spirit remains in the people, this can produce quite a prideful striving.

The Spirit of competition needs to be taken out of the heart, and it is this anointing that really does it. After the Lord had spoken to me about this 'anointing by which community is built', I came to realise that this must be strongly related to the revelation I had been given some years earlier where He spoke to me about *understanding*. I have come to see that this 'anointing by which community is built' is called *the spirit of understanding*.

This is one of the seven graces that rested upon the Christ, spoken of by the prophet Isaiah in Isaiah 11:2, and is specifically the anointing that, amongst other things, causes people to be of one heart and one mind. Without that anointing we cannot be of one heart and one mind, because this is the anointing that displaces the spirit of competition from our hearts. Why it is called 'understanding' I will discuss later.

If rocks are placed into a bucket full of water, the bucket will hold less water as rocks are added. If sand is poured in among the rocks, there is less room still for water. This is displacement, and illustrates what happens in the human heart when this anointing comes in. The spirit of understanding takes the place of the spirit of competition. This completely changes the hearts of believers so that they see each other, and the work of God, with different eyes, because their hearts have been changed by grace. Instead of living out of a believing heart still influenced by striving, they now see each other and the church as a whole from a different perspective, because of a grace called understanding now established in them.

Two: Admiration of One Another

Once this spirit of understanding has come in, there is a state of peace established out of which love, acceptance, and appreciation flows. The stronger word for this is *admiration*. Like the Moravians, the Church must become *a people who greatly admire each other.* A 'mutual admiration society' may sound humorous, but is merely another way of saying what Paul said, *"Honour one another above yourselves,"* and what Jesus said – *"Love one another, as I have loved you."* This is, in fact, what love really is. And it becomes established in us the same way it did at Pentecost, and with the Moravians – by an anointing, i.e. a work of grace. A gift for it must be given by the Holy Spirit.

A Mutual Admiration Society!

Every local church should be *a mutual admiration society*. This is the opposite thing to the striving we often see. It was said of the early church that the Christians greatly loved each other. It was often the enemies of the church that made that observation. A mutual admiration society indeed!

Mutual Admiration

Scripture says we are to *"accept one another as Christ has accepted us."* (Romans 15: 7) Christ finds us acceptable because He has made us acceptable, and we are meant to have the same 'view' of each other. Jesus loves you, admires you, and finds you acceptable. The Scripture says that you are acceptable to God in Christ, and that Christ accepted you to bring praise to God. Your brothers and sisters are also accepted in Christ, and since Jesus so admires you, and them, you need to admire the other believers as He does.

Let me illustrate what I find fascinating about genuine love. The people in life that love me the most are the ones who admire me the most. Who are these people? They are the people who are closest to me, my wife and children. They have a big heart for me and I have a big heart for them. We love one another to the point where we stick together, admiring each other. I admire my wife more than anyone, and she admires me more than anyone. But notice something unusual. The people who admire and love me the most, are the same people who are the most familiar with my faults and failings – such as the times I am impatient, the mistakes I make, the times I get angry and have to be sorry about it afterwards, the times when I misunderstand someone – it is my wife and children who have a grandstand seat to these things, as I do to theirs—yet they are the ones who admire me the most and love without question.

What does this prove? It proves that in the church, knowing each other's faults and weaknesses is not a barrier to admiring other people. In a mutual admiration society, our love and admiration for others is not based on their perfection or performance. It is based upon what is in our heart toward them.

When the church is full of genuine love, it will be full of admiration. I have heard agape love preached with a definition which falls short of what I think Bible love is. We were often told that you don't have to like people, but you do have to love them. Whilst there is truth there, this could also be cold love, which Jesus said would be a danger at the end of the age. (Matthew 24: 12)

We were often told that if you have agape love, you don't have to have *feelings* for people, but you act in accordance with their higher good. There is a lot of truth in that, in so far as no matter how we feel, we should act in accordance with the principle of love. But we should never make that an excuse for not having feelings in the church. We are meant to be a people of deep feelings, because God is a Person of deep feelings.

When Paul said farewell to the Ephesian elders, he told them, "*I know that none of you... will ever see me again.*" (Acts 20: 25) They would not stop weeping and holding on to him because their feelings, the genuine emotion of their hearts, were so deep. That is consistent with true church leadership. The apostle Paul and the elders loved each other to the point of tears. Such deep affection! And that is what Biblical Christianity is. Paul wrote to Timothy saying, "*Recalling your tears, I long to see you, that I may be filled with joy.*" (2 Timothy 1: 4) He would not have been making it up.

The anointing we are speaking of makes a great difference to our feelings, just as it did for the Moravians. They didn't become a people who *merely* loved each other; they became a people who *admired* each other. We too will be a mutual admiration society when our hearts are made big enough by the grace of God.

Now it is not a question of whether just a few people can love each other well. The question is, can the whole congregation love each other? Is there a grace that will change everyone's heart? This is in fact what the revelation of "understanding" points to. The Lord said if He could put the spirit of understanding upon a people it would totally change their life. They would become a people of one heart and one mind, they would rise as one man, and they would do God's work in the world. Nothing would be able to resist them, and their lives would be totally transformed.

This is the Grace of Understanding

With the Moravians, none of this was contrived. No one was pushed into conformity. Each was free, but grace gave them a heart for each other. Can we say this loudly and clearly – it is a gift!! And God is able to give such gifts, in answer to prayer.

CHAPTER-SIX

UNDERSTANDING AS AN *Anointing* HOW DOES IT WORK?

"The Spirit of the Lord will rest upon him –
The Spirit of wisdom and of understanding,
The Spirit of counsel and of power,
The Spirit of knowledge and of the fear of the Lord –
And he will delight in the fear of the Lord."
Isaiah 11: 2-3a

The instructions of Christ through His apostles tell us to honour one another above ourselves, to accept one another as Christ has accepted us, that our love must be without hypocrisy, and that we are to love one another deeply from the heart. These things are often preached, but not as often fulfilled, because we have not known how to fulfil them. The truth is, not only do we need to believe in these values of the heart, what we really need is power to live this way. We need a grace that transforms; we need power to enable the work. And the spirit of understanding is that needed grace.

But how does this anointing called 'the Spirit of understanding' actually work?

Jesus was born as a baby with no special knowledge. He needed to grow and learn the significance of who He was. (Luke 2:52) He had to become perfected in His understanding and obedience so that He would be perfect in His suffering. This little baby, who knew nothing except to look for His mother's milk, was completely dependent on His mother and father to look after Him. He had a human brain in a human body.

How did He become the person He was meant to be? How was He brought through everything, so that even at the age of 12, He is recorded as saying, *"Didn't you know I had to be in my Father's house?"* At other times He said variously, *"I and the Father are one – Anyone who has seen me has seen the Father – The Son can do nothing by himself; he can do only what he sees his Father doing – my judgment is just, for I seek not to please myself but him who sent me."* (John 10: 30, 14: 9, 5: 19, 5: 30) How could He be so one with the Father? And what made this possible when He was in the flesh? There is an answer to these questions – it was made possible by the Spirit of God upon Him, so that by grace He was enabled to live the way He lived, rather than because of any human ability.

There were seven anointings upon Him. These anointings were prophesied seven hundred years before He was born; I am referring to Isaiah 11: 2. The workings of these anointings explain many things. Jesus was given these anointings without limit (John 3: 34-35), but you and I have just a portion of them. In some cases, people have very little indeed, but more is available. These anointings are the key to seeing the life of the church transformed; whatever rested upon Jesus is meant to rest upon the body of Christ.

This is what Isaiah said. "*The Spirit of the Lord will rest upon Him.*" That's the first anointing. But Isaiah moves on. He says, "*the Spirit of wisdom and of understanding, the Spirit of counsel and of power, the Spirit of knowledge and of the fear of the Lord - and he will delight in the fear of the Lord.*" We should see these as seven specific anointings, and it is possible to define what each of these does.[1] But we must also understand that in Christ these anointings were not divisible; one could not be separated from the other. We must see this as a seamless grace, where all the anointings present are joined as if one great anointing. This is also a possible state of grace for the church.

The Seven-fold Spirit

There are various places in the Bible where the Holy Spirit is referred to as the seven-fold Spirit. Translations have some difficulty with this. Is it "the seven spirits of God," or is it the one spirit with seven aspects? Often the translation will be the "seven-fold Spirit."

Revelation 1:4-5 is a passage about the triune God. The text refers to God, to the Son, and to the Spirit. "*Grace and peace to you from Him who is, and who was, and who is to come, and from the seven spirits before His throne, and*

1 A free Audio message explaining the purpose of each of the seven anointings is available for download at www.peace.org.au - Go to Audio Files, and look for the title, "The Seven Anointings of Jesus Christ."

from Jesus Christ, who is the faithful witness..." The "seven spirits of God" is a reference to the Holy Spirit. In Revelation 3:1 Jesus is speaking. "*To the angel of the church in Sardis write: These are the words of Him who holds the seven spirits of God and the seven stars..."* So we see a repeated emphasis in Scripture to there being some seven aspects to the life of the Spirit as it is revealed to us.

The third of these seven anointings, the Spirit of Understanding, was the grace by which the Son was one with the Father during His days on earth. In fact it would be true to say that this is the very life the members of the Godhead share in walking with one another. They share the grace of understanding. Jesus was not automatically controlled from heaven as if He were some kind of robot or computer. He was not pre-programmed. He had to live his life every day by walking with God. And yet He could say, "*I always do what pleases Him.*" (John 8:29) The depth of this grace in Jesus' heart gave Him such understanding that not only did He know the heart of God the Father, but He had the same heart.

Jesus *understood* who He was, and who the Father was. He understood righteousness and the will of God, and He freely and lovingly sought to do the will of God. And when the spirit of understanding is given to churches, and the contrary spirit removed, it makes all the difference in how the people walk together and work together. They are far more likely to see and feel the same way about things.

It is a grace. Grace, by its nature, is something that does not have to be deserved: it is given freely by God. And when we receive grace, we always receive power; that too is the nature of grace.

One of the vital aspects of the grace of God is being able to be truly one with another person, as we see in the Holy Trinity; a power that is largely lacking in the church. We see churches with division. We see striving, ambition, and struggle, usually because there is a missing grace which we need to obtain for our churches.

In the Bible there are four words that can often be used interchangeably; grace, spirit, power, and anointing. For example, in the book of Numbers we have a story where God, referring to the seventy-two elders, speaks to Moses and says, *"...I will take of the spirit that is on you and put the Spirit on them..."* (Numbers 11:17)

Why would God take the Spirit that was on Moses? Why did God not just give them the Holy Spirit? In order to understand this, we need to see that we are talking about an anointing – one which had been given to Moses to lead the people. God was not going to give another 72 men a separate anointing, for leadership of the same group, independent from the one He had given Moses. They had to have a portion of the *same* anointing so as to be part of a whole, and subject to the authority of Moses. This passage says 'spirit', but what we're dealing with is the giving of a grace. Moses had power to lead, he had the grace to lead, and that's what an anointing is; it is God giving someone a grace by which they will have the power to do things they need to do. This is called an anointing, and is given by the Holy Spirit. Now you can see how these four words interplay.

Here is another example. In Luke 1, the angel came to Zechariah and spoke of John the Baptist. *"And he will go on before the Lord, in the spirit and power of Elijah..."* In other words, the same grace that was given to Elijah was to be given to John the Baptist. John the Baptist would have the same anointing as Elijah, so that he could accomplish the same things.

And the New Testament tells us that Jesus ministered from *anointings*. Acts 10: 37-38 says, *"You know... how God anointed Jesus of Nazareth with the Holy Spirit and power, and how he went around doing good and healing all who were under the power of the devil, because God was with him."* Even Jesus needed anointings. What Jesus did, He did by the grace that was given.

Part of that grace was for Christ to be one with the Father, and that particular grace is meant to be upon each of our congregations as a very present anointing, so that in the same way that Jesus was one with the Father, we too may be one with each other. This precisely is what Jesus prayed our fellowship would be like, in His prayer recorded in John 17: 21.

And this particular grace, or anointing, is called *the Spirit of Understanding*.

It is amazing how often the word 'understanding' occurs in the Scriptures, and how much the Bible has to say about it.

In Colossians 2:2-3 Paul wrote: *"My purpose is that they may be encouraged in heart and united in love, so that they may have the full riches of complete understanding, in order that they may know the mystery of God, namely, Christ, in whom are hidden all the treasures of wisdom and knowledge."* In the middle of this long sentence is a reference to the mystery of God, namely Christ! We are here urged to obtain the full riches of complete *understanding*, so as to have a true and deep knowledge of this person who is in Himself the mystery of God revealed.

But notice there is something else required by which you may gain this understanding. It is stated that we need to be united in love, i.e. the church must be united in love so as to have the full riches of understanding. And if we have the fullness of understanding, we will then have the full revelation of Jesus Christ.

These three things are connected; all the rich treasures of Christ are connected to the spirit of understanding, which is connected to being united in love. This phase, *"united in love"* certainly indicates the shared life we are urged to experience in the church.

When understanding as an anointing is given into the heart and mind of believers, people *see*, people *know*, people *discern*, people *understand!* Believers are far more likely to love the same things, and therefore choose the same things. In the heart will be a deeper sense of and love for the ways of God, and a greater discernment about what is right and holy – and all in the context of any striving against one another being removed.

This grace was pure in Jesus, i.e. there was no other spirit in Him. And it can be this way for us, too. And when oneness of spirit is given to a body of believers, they have a relationship which is not just partnership, not just cooperation, and not just agreement, but *oneness*.

Oneness is the real meaning of the word unity. Psalm 133, written long ago, expressed the heart of God: *"How good and pleasant it is when brothers live together in unity."* The Psalm goes on to equate this situation, of believers in complete unity, with the pouring out of the Holy Spirit, with the anointing of the high priest, with an abundant provision of the dew of heaven (a symbol of the Holy Spirit coming upon the earth), and upon this oneness comes the commanded blessing.

Following are two stories that illustrate the anointing at work.

A few years ago I went to Cambodia to spend some days in a retreat with 150 pastors and wives. I had been to teach the same group the year before, when I had covered a variety of subjects, including grace and listening prayer, with just one lecture on the apostolic reformation of the church. Although they seemed to take hold of the other subjects well, they did not seem to grasp the apostolic message in any appreciable way.

I knew that on this second occasion, I was to teach them about apostolic grace in every session, which would include such things as father-son relationship, the unity of the body, city eldership, and community.

In the opening meeting when it was time to speak, I purposely began with a very specific prayer. Remembering other occasions when by grace I had been able to bring anointings upon meetings, I prayed and by faith took hold of the spirit of understanding and brought it down upon the meeting. In the name of the Lord Jesus, I released the anointing to the hearts and minds of these Cambodian men and women. In that moment a wonderful thing occurred. The power of God came, invisibly, through the solid brick wall on my right, and flooded over the whole meeting. The proof was in the fact that the gathering absolutely came to life with understanding the messages I then brought over the next three days. They hung on to the words, and the message went deep to the heart. There were many testimonies, and tears, and it was very clear that a great grace had been given to those people.

On another occasion, in Tasmania, Australia, I was invited to speak to a joint meeting of the pastors and leadership teams of three churches, a group of about fifty. It was a Monday night, and they gave me two hours to teach. I gave a wide-ranging lecture connecting a number of related subjects together, after which I prayed for them.

Nine months later I was back in the same city for an apostolic conference. One of the lectures I gave, late in the conference, was on the subject of this book. After completing the session, I got talking to the senior pastor of one of those three churches, who had been sitting in the front row. It was his building we had the meeting in nine months before, and he had something he wanted to tell me. "John," he said. "You taught us about that community anointing when you were with us nine months ago, and afterwards you prayed and released that anointing to the people who were present. I want you to know that since that night, my whole church has been different."

There is power in anointings, obviously, but what is less obvious to some is that we are meant to have an anointing for everything we do for Christ. In fact, the point of view of the Scriptures is that work done without an anointing is not acceptable to God, because it is flesh.

Understanding as an anointing brings about unity (which includes love and acceptance of one another), not by forcing conformity, but by putting into the heart and mind the ability to see things and feel things God's way, while at the same time the striving that would usually either distract us or drive us, is much diminished or removed. It is a great grace, and community cannot be built without it.

CHAPTER-SEVEN

A More Complete *Pentecost*

"It is for your good that I am going away.
Unless I go away, the Counselor will not come to you;
but if I go, I will send Him to you."

John 16: 7

There were not many things the disciples of Jesus could do after Pentecost that they didn't do before, but they sure stopped doing after Pentecost what they did a lot of before. They stopped arguing with each other. In 1 Corinthians 1:10, Paul spoke of the need for believers to be "*perfectly united in mind and thought.*" Wherever that occurs, it will be the direct fruit of Pentecost.

I do not mean this in a general sense, as if it is an automatic outcome for Christians who, after all, do each have a measure of the Holy Spirit within, but rather as a direct result of specifically receiving this Pentecostal anointing. True, there are 'Pentecostal' churches everywhere that do not have this oneness of mind and thought, but this nevertheless remains the New Testament picture of what pentecostal grace provides for.

Think about it again. Aside from the gift of tongues, what was the only thing the early believers had after Pentecost that was different from before? It was not miracle-working power; even before Pentecost, Jesus had been sending out large numbers of believers with authority over every kind of sickness and disease and over demonic powers. He breathed on them and said, *"Receive the Holy Spirit."* (John 20: 22) He opened their minds to understand Scripture (Luke 24: 45). With the exception of tongues, the things which we consider in today's terms to be the effect of Pentecost were being experienced and practiced by the believers in some measure prior to Pentecost. No, Pentecost gave them something else.

Before and After

Prior to Pentecost, whenever they thought Jesus wasn't listening, the disciples were often to be found arguing among themselves, specifically about which of them was the greatest. But after the day of Pentecost, they did not think that way any longer. Before Pentecost, the believers consisted of people who, whilst being followers of Jesus, were not especially connected to each other. There was a form of community built around and specifically centred on Jesus, but the individuals were still pretty much independent of one another.

Unfortunately, that is what we find today – churches, including many Pentecostal churches, with a pre-Pentecost experience of church life.

Many of these gather together as the church because they believe the gospel and are following Christ. They believe the Word of God, and desire to do what Jesus requires of them. They gather to worship Jesus, and they are gathering for Jesus' sake. We often say that the thing that binds us together is our love for Jesus, and that is wonderful, but Biblically, that is not enough.

In fact, to say that the only thing that binds us together is our love for Jesus is a false gospel, because of the astounding thing that happened on the day of Pentecost. The Holy Spirit came, and His coming as the promised Gift of God made a phenomenal change in the Church. No longer were they only in love with Jesus; they were in love with each other as well. They no longer had merely an outward form of community based on the fact that they were all followers of Jesus. Now it was genuine community, because the power they had been given not only established a living connection to the resurrected, ascended Jesus, but also a dynamic, effective heart connection to each other. This was love, and this was the work of the Holy Spirit; to make them, and us in turn, one.

During the three years of Jesus' ministry when He lived among the people, many were gathered to Him. Not just the 12, or the 72; there were 120 in the upper room, and He had appeared to 500 believers after His resurrection. There were many people whose lives revolved around Jesus. To be properly connected to Jesus is the first step in the Christian faith, so we see that Jesus formed community consisting of each person with Himself, but they were not yet connected to each other. This is what the Holy Spirit was to do.

These individual believers loved Jesus, served Jesus, and were willing to die for Jesus, but after the day of Pentecost, when these believers were joined to each other as well, we find they loved the brethren, served the brethren, and were willing to lay down their lives for the brethren. This is a major, significant change. And it is something in Pentecost that does this, not only then, but now. If our experience of church life is not this big, then we need to find the real Pentecost; and we need to preach the availability of a bigger and more far-reaching baptism of the Spirit.

Only the Holy Spirit is able to take a group of people, unwilling and unable to be joined together, and make them one. A good word to define the human condition is 'disparate' – a term which means that not only are we separated from each other, but we are quite unable to be joined together due to extreme differences of kind, i.e. the parts don't match and don't fit. Yet the Holy Spirit is able to take disparate believers and make them *one*. That was, and remains, the primary purpose of Pentecost above all others. In the case of those first disciples, their differences were evident right up until the day of Pentecost when the Spirit was poured out. No wonder Jesus had said, *"It is for your good that I am going away. Unless I go away, the Counselor will not come to you; but if I go, I will send Him to you."* (John 16: 7)

The gift of tongues is so powerfully effective and valuable when used properly, it deserves to be held in high view and not done without – but it is not the primary purpose of Pentecost so far as being an end in itself. The baptism of the Holy Spirit brings with it great authority and gifting, as well as a renewed life in the Word of God, but if these are the only evidences of Pentecost we experience, then we are still poorer than we should be. There is more to the baptism of the Spirit, and it is meant to take us somewhere *together*.

Acts 4:32 states, *"All the believers were one in heart and mind......"* This description was of the church some time after the outpouring of the Holy Spirit in Acts 2, and by this time there were thousands of believers. Yet the Scriptures say that *all* of the people were one in heart and mind. These believers had both the unity of the Spirit and the unity of the faith. What caused this? The community anointing of Pentecost did. "Understanding" had been poured into them.

In all the mighty works of the grace of God, Pentecost always had the one central purpose – to form community; to take people who were not joined together and make them one people. In the Bible, there are two Pentecosts; one in the Old Testament and one in the New Testament. Pentecost was an important part of both Old and New covenants.

The Pentecost of the Old Testament

The Old Covenant Pentecost occurred with the giving of the law at Mount Sinai. At that original Pentecost, the 'mixed multitude' of slaves (they were not all Jacob's descendants, nor even Abraham's) who came out of Egypt was declared to be a nation – and holy unto the Lord. That is, they became, at least symbolically, no longer disparate but a *community*. They were to be *a people*.

The Old had shortcomings, for there was death under the law, and its primary purpose anyway was to be a shadow and type for what was to come later; but the New Pentecost was to have the fullness of life in Christ. At the time of that

Old Pentecost three thousand died (Exodus 32: 28), but on the day of the New Covenant Pentecost three thousand were saved, as recorded in Acts 2: 41. The Old Pentecost was external, pertaining to things that could be seen and heard and touched. The community formed was outward, i.e. physical in nature. Everything about the Old was physical, outward, material – and temporary.

We have been given something better – a better covenant with better promises. We have a better High Priest, a better blood, and a better priesthood. We have a better law (the law of love), a better way of approaching God, a better everything. (See Hebrews 7:11 – 9:28)

The New Testament Pentecost

When the Spirit of God came on the early church in Jerusalem as a result of the new Covenant in Christ's blood, the central, primary anointing was this anointing for community, and all other gifts, graces, and anointings were attached to it. All the gifts of tongues and prophecy, all the power for miracles, and every other quickening, blessing, and favour from God came attached to this anointing for community. All these were specifically attached to community because if community is not formed, if Christ's followers are not *a body*, if the fellowship is in name only, then the gifts and graces do not have a wineskin, a culture, a holy reservoir, out of which to operate properly for the advance of the Kingdom of Christ. It is this anointing for community that is meant to transform how we see each other, how we feel about each other, and how we walk together. This anointing puts love in the heart, so that we are truly then one people for Christ's sake.

The point again is that the purpose of Pentecost is always

to bring a 'mixed multitude', a disparate people, into community – to cause people who are not one to be one. Whereas in the Old Testament it was physical, external, heavily symbolic, and temporary, in the New Testament it is internal, spiritual, of the heart, real, and eternal.

This is why, when groups of Christians go through all the external motions, with a building to meet in on Sunday mornings, some agreement about the work they will do, and holding to a common doctrine, it is not enough. All these things can be merely external in nature, and the inferior Old Covenant used to get people that far. The one really big difference under the New Covenant is the giving of the Spirit, and every Christian group, fellowship, or church needs the undiluted benefit that came with this grace gift – namely, oneness.

We must see Pentecost as the *outpouring* (i.e. the unrestrained giving) of everything that we need; of every gift, grace, and anointing the Father has for us. Therefore every anointing, including the seven primary graces that rested without measure on the Christ, has been given in Pentecost and remains available for the church. But please understand: whilst every (and therefore numerous) anointings were poured out, there is a *central* anointing to which all others are connected – and there is a primary *purpose*, to which all other desired goals or outcomes are attached. An explosion of love is the goal of the *central* anointing of Pentecost. If we receive tongues but not a greater love, then whilst we have received something good, we have missed out on the great grace of the central anointing. (1 Cor 13: 1)

For years we have made the mistake of preaching Pentecost as an *individual* experience. Our thinking was that each believer can be baptised in the Holy Spirit, can speak in tongues, can heal the sick, and can win souls. "One man with Christ is a majority, so go out in the power of the Spirit, and conquer the world for Jesus!" is the kind of thing commonly enough thought, and preached. In thinking like this, we might have in mind a picture of someone like Elijah (although this is to misunderstand Elijah), and totally miss the main message of the New Testament – that we are meant to be of one heart and mind with all the believers – and together speak with one voice. (See Romans 15: 5-7)

John, the apostle of love, opens his first epistle by saying: *"We proclaim to you what we have seen and heard, so that you also may have fellowship with us. And our fellowship is with the Father and with his Son, Jesus Christ."* (1 John 1:3) What was it they heard, saw, and touched? It was Jesus. John recorded that the reason he proclaimed Jesus to them was, "*so that you also may have fellowship with us.*"

We miss the full gospel when we miss the "us". There are many who claim to preach a "full gospel"; but here we find that the gospel is a little bigger and fuller than we thought. Even if we didn't miss the gospel, we do miss the bulk of Pentecost when we miss the "us".

We could even go so far as to ask: If a group of believers is not in love with each other, can they be called Pentecostals? And if a church is not in community, is it really in Pentecost?

The Baptism of the Spirit

In 1974, after great hunger in prayer, I personally experienced late one night a life-changing baptism of the Holy Spirit – with tongues, authority over unclean spirits, revelation in the Word of God, and best of all, an amazing catapult into a great security in the love of God – and I have preached it ever since. But like perhaps many others, I taught the baptism of the Spirit inaccurately, for we have been preaching it, as I said before, as an individualistic experience of God.

In the same way that every individual is to be born again, we preach that every individual is to be baptised in the Holy Spirit. So far, so good. But when we say that they can have the power of God, and can prophesy and heal the sick, and can win souls, and can go out and take the world for Jesus (all of which is true enough in the right context with the right values), we often have just reinforced the "American dream" (You know, one man, by working hard, can rise to the top, etc…). This has often, I think, unintentionally reinforced rugged individualism in the church, and it was never intended for that.

Thus we presented the grace of God to believers in a way that permitted their independence, and so they kept their individualism, believing in themselves, "their" calling, and "their" ministry. There was no antidote in our doctrine of the power of the Spirit to striving and competition. But now, empowered by the truth and this anointing, we must change things. We must teach our people that there is something even bigger and more wonderful in their Holy Spirit baptism.

A Little History

The Pentecostal movement which started just over a hundred years ago has been an amazing and wonderful work of God that has changed the whole church. But it is not the whole of what God ultimately wants to do. It is only one stage in what God has been doing to ready us for the thing He is bringing us to. We all have to move on.

But fifty years prior to Azusa Street there was another great move of the Spirit which, commencing in the East End of London, became known as The Salvation Army. Their founder, William Booth, urged upon his followers to seek and obtain what he called, "The mighty Pentecostal baptism of the Holy Spirit." They would spend whole nights crying out to God for this mighty baptism of the power of the Spirit. And they didn't necessarily believe that this was a once-only experience; they were hungry enough, and in prayer enough, to be baptised with power all over again. The Holy Spirit would fall with tremendous power in their all-night prayer meetings, and there would be wonderful scenes of great liberty in which they would dance, and cry out for joy, and be laid out on the floor under the moving of the Spirit of God. There were phenomenal scenes of great power. But they had a particular belief about what was received in the baptism of the Spirit, which I will come to in a moment.

Pentecostals also have beliefs about what is received in a baptism of the Spirit. They believe they will speak in tongues, and possibly do other things as well, such as prophesy or heal the sick. So we have had 100 years in which the baptism of the Spirit has been mainly associated with spiritual giftedness. But the Salvation Army had a different belief. They believed that when the baptism of the Holy Spirit was given, you were given two things in particular: power to live a holy life, and the power to win souls.

And these are the two things in which The Salvation Army really excelled. You will never read more heart-moving and unusual stories of lives lived for Christ than of those early founders of The Salvation Army – stories of courageous men and amazing women who lived such holy lives. And the Salvation Army, in spreading to 80 nations in 25 years, brought millions of people to Christ. William Booth, from one evangelist, became 10,000 evangelists. They believed that the baptism of the Spirit would give them power to win souls, and they won souls everywhere they went. They were totally unique.

Later Azusa Street opened up completely new dimensions for all believers, which should always be added to what was there before, but wc tend to forget. And here I am saying there is yet another dimension to Pentecost as well. Yes, it was there all along, and is, after all, the single-most important dimension – the powerful grace for community.

My point in recounting history is this: you will get what you believe for. Whatever it is that you believe is in the baptism of the Spirit, you will likely receive when you wait upon God for it. Why not believe for it all?

When we teach converts, or the church as a whole, we must tell them the truth: the main reason for the baptism of the Spirit is to cause you to become of one heart and one mind with the believers. The church is going to be a powerful people together – we have power to live holy lives together, and power to win souls together – and this power comes with all the gifts of the Holy Spirit, so we are a powerfully gifted people together.

Preaching a Bigger Pentecost

For this last 100 years, Pentecost has been largely about the gifts of the Spirit. The Pentecostal/charismatic movement all over the world has been a phenomenal grace for God's people. We have around 450-500 million believers whose lives have been transformed by the power of the Spirit. The baptism of the Spirit has been a great success story for the Kingdom of God.

But where do we go now? Is “Azusa Street” the last big thing that God will ever do? And now, after that, do we just get little variations on the theme? I think not. God is still in the business of doing mighty deeds. We are thankful for what He has done in the past, but we can’t live for the past; we need to enjoy the blessings established in the past, but live for what God wants to do now.

A leader at the Bible College I attended was fond of saying, “God hasn’t done His best thing yet.” What does that mean? If you define God’s best thing in terms of Christ and Calvary, there is no competing with that. But in terms of what God does in history with the lives of men and women, and His dealings with churches and people groups, we are not to think that God has already done all the great things and now we are just to live on in the light of that.

The God I know is not the kind who did His best thing first, and then all He could do next was His second best thing, and after that His third best thing, and so on. Otherwise, we might be looking back on Azusa Street or something else and thinking that was the best thing God ever did, and having a second class hope for our own times and those of our children.

In the past God raised many mighty servants; unusual ones like Samson, astounding prophets like Samuel and Isaiah and Jeremiah, apostles like Peter, James, John, and Paul. There were men and women through all the centuries who performed great deeds, brought forth great truths, changed history, and like Patrick in Ireland, conquered whole lands for Christ. Do you think whole nations can no longer be conquered? But if God hasn’t done His best thing yet, it means He will yet raise even more great men and women. There are yet to be great revivals, and more great outpourings of the Spirit. And, I think, greater apostles and prophets must yet come!

I thank God for what He has done in the last hundred years, for the great Welsh revival, for Azusa Street, for the charismatic renewal, for the Toronto blessing, and everything else that occurred in between. I thank God for the restoration of the five-fold ministry, and for prophets and apostles. But all these previous moves of the Spirit were meeting the needs of the Body of Christ at that time, as well as moving us on and positioning us for the future. Right now, we must believe that God has something even better planned, and there are yet to be greater works done in this world.

We should now be contemplating what we are to look for. We are in the early years of a new century, and I think we have something great to anticipate, and work for. The grace of Pentecost will bring about truly great works and victories for Christ all over the world. Nations and people groups will be transformed. Community has the power to do this.

May I Say In Summary:

Real Christianity is based on Relationships

True Christianity is based on relationships, with believers being built together and sharing a common life. This is the life given to the Church when baptised by the Holy Spirit on the day of Pentecost. To be a Pentecostal is to walk in that life. The Lord is bringing the church into maturity, and no church is mature unless it is mature in relationships. No Christian is spiritually mature unless they are relationally mature. Pentecost gives us the power to build those relationships.

A Real Pentecost produces Relationships

If the spirit of Pentecost is in your heart, it will cause you to love your brothers and sisters, and to be one with all the saints. That is the primary purpose of Pentecost. The purpose of the Gift of the Spirit was to take people who believed in Jesus and join them so they could be of one heart and mind, able to speak with one voice, and rise as one to do the works of God.

For the Century Ahead - Community!

In the last hundred years, Pentecost was seen as a powerful work of the Holy Spirit in individual believers. For the next 'hundred years'(and without forgetting what we already have), Pentecost will be seen and worked out as the powerful work of the Holy Spirit in and through 'apostolic companies' of believers who are in the powerful union of Christ-like communities. Why? One of the reasons is that Christ is bringing the church to maturity before the great day of the coming of our Lord – and this requires the bride to be made spotless by love.

We will need to preach the Baptism of the Holy Spirit, with the *ongoing* evidence of believers being in community.

CHAPTER-EIGHT

THE *Necessity* OF TEACHING VALUES

"... make my joy complete by being like-minded,
having the same love,
being one in spirit and purpose.

Do nothing out of selfish ambition or vain conceit,
but in humility consider others better than yourselves.
Each of you should look not only to your own interests,
but also to the interests of others.

Your attitude should be the same as that of Christ Jesus;
Who, being in very nature God,
did not consider equality with God something to be grasped,
but made himself nothing,
taking the very nature of a servant,
being made in human likeness.
And being found in appearance as a man,
he humbled himself and became obedient to death –
even death on a cross!"

Philippians 2:2-8

So far, I have emphasized that the key to building community is a *power* key, and that it is not possible to create community without the anointing to do so.

But the anointing spoken of is only one of *two* things that are completely necessary to build effective Christian community. The other, also much needed, is the teaching of the *values* of Christian community, by consistent leadership devoted to this very important role.

In a nutshell, there you have it. Creating community requires both right *values* to be in the heart, and the *power* of grace to come upon those who believe these values. Thus will the believers have power to live in accordance with their principles and convictions, and having the right values will have prepared them for what the Holy Spirit gives them.

Much has been shared about the power of Pentecost in making the early church a people of one heart. But this did not happen in a vacuum, i.e. it did not happen to a people unprepared. Prior to Pentecost, Jesus did not only work miracles, and send others out to do the same. He spent much time teaching, and especially, teaching His disciples. And what He taught, more than anything else, was values.

Jesus Taught Values for 3 Years before Pentecost

For three years, Jesus taught not just the twelve, or the seventy, but hundreds of others. He was putting into them the things they needed to believe about how they should live, and think, and feel, even if they were not able to come to grips with these things. His teaching, like the following examples, would have seemed difficult and other-worldly to them: *"A new command I give you: love one another. As I have loved you, so you must love one another."* (John 13:34)

"The greatest among you will be your servant." (Matthew 23:11) "....whoever welcomes a little child like this in my name welcomes me." (Matthew 18:5)

In all this and more, Jesus was teaching values; how to *think* and what to believe. And were the disciples much better at loving one another after this teaching? No, they were just like every believer sitting in church for many years who hears teaching that we must love one another. We all know we are meant to love one another – and we believe it from the heart – but just as often we are not very good at doing it. This is because it is then necessary to add power to the teaching of beliefs and values.

And teaching values is exactly what Jesus did, but then, after teaching for three years, He told the disciples, *".....It is for your good that I am going away. Unless I go away, the Counselor will not come to you; but if I go, I will send him to you."* (John 16:7) Here Jesus was speaking of the coming of the grace and power that would be placed upon the values they had learned.

How Values Work

A value is what people believe in their hearts. It is not so much what they say they believe; it is what they believe deep down – often their real beliefs are subconscious. People will always act out of their values, and that is why, sometimes, someone will say one thing, but do another. Whenever anybody acts in some strange, unusual or unexpected way, I will always say to my staff, they are acting in accordance with something they believe in their heart. The way Christians act, the way they conduct themselves in the household of God, will always be in keeping with what they somehow, right or wrong, believe.

We will say all kinds of things about what we think we believe, but for every few dozen beliefs we are aware of, we have perhaps hundreds of beliefs tucked away in another place altogether, and it is from these that we actually live, i.e. we usually act, react, and speak out of hidden beliefs, which form attitudes. These are our values. In the heart we believe certain things to be incontrovertibly true, and out of those we act.

Amongst these are what you believe about yourself, for example. Also, what you believe about your wife or your husband, what you believe about the church, what you believe about your children, the pastor, the day in which you live, etc. We are filled with beliefs, but most of these we don't actually annunciate, but live out of them all the while.

How can we identify what we actually believe? Very often we can do so by what we *feel*. In various circumstances we feel agreement, uncertainties, caution, fear, boldness, anger, etc. All of these can be a signal pointing to what our heart values are.

We have generations of Christians all around us, older and younger, many of whom have grown up in denominational or institutional expressions of Christianity of one kind or another. They are filled with beliefs about the nature of Christianity, and the nature of the church, how the church should be governed and led, and so on. They have beliefs about what you can do, and what you can't do, in the church. Basically they have many, invisible, pre-formed attitudes, many of which are values held dear.

Most of us, without realising it, have within a store of institutional values, traditions as values, and often enough, other kinds of narrow-minded values too. That is where the spirit of poverty can also find a home. And it's many of these values that have to change to embrace the benefits of a real, apostolic, relational church life.

Dr William Beckham, a Christian teacher who travelled extensively teaching Cell Church concepts, used to regularly say, "People do what they value, and they value what they do!" This is why it is essential that we teach right values in a holy endeavour to *change* whatever values the believers hold that are contrary to the way of Christ and the direction He wants for the church as a people together.

The church generally, as a result of five hundred years of denominationalised Protestantism, some of which was built on medieval Catholicism anyway, has ended up with a whole set of institutionalised values that are not apostolic, i.e. not especially Christian in the New Testament sense.

Often the denominational institution is valued more than the key leader the Lord has put there to love, lead, and protect the believers who are gathered in that institution (to use an extreme illustration, that would be a bit like valuing the golden calf more than Moses, the man of God). Consequently, you get many situations where, once there is division in a local church, the denomination will put the pastor aside, or move him/her along, even though they did nothing wrong, and more often than not the pastor was probably right in representing Christ bringing in some change. It is not uncommon that the people who opposed were out of order, falsely accusing, or trying to maintain control politically. The denomination will often not support the pastor, but instead side with the political ringleaders, so as to 'save' that church, and its financial support, as part of their own organisation. This is a vile corruption, but is often the way of institutionalised Christianity. This is a product of wrong values, because all or most of these people will have acted in accordance with what they *believe* is right. The belief systems are awry, and the values misplaced.

Therefore we are, by necessity, in the process of re-educating people. Hopefully, we are causing people to think. In past years, I have led many conferences in which the Holy Spirit would fall with power, take over sessions, and people all over the room would be caught up in the move of the Spirit, sometimes with unusual manifestations of His prophetic word or His presence. However, when the Lord sent me to teach about apostolic grace, those manifestations rarely occurred in the meetings. No one was to be distracted from the teaching of the apostolic message by such experiences – theirs or others – for the Lord was now dealing with what people were *thinking*.

We need to teach thoroughly the appropriate, apostolic, relational values that Jesus, and later the apostles, taught – and the New Testament is full of it. Thus we are in the process of changing the values of the church – changing how people think, what they believe, and in particular, changing what we believe about each other – and even more especially, changing what we believe about our leaders. We have to consistently lay the conceptual foundations for community.

We didn't realise it at the time, but just as Jesus had taught His disciples for three years before they were ready to receive the full benefit of Pentecost, we taught our church for seven years – and this must have helped prepare us for the day when the Lord finally said, "There is an anointing…"

It sounds like it was a long task for us, but when you are trying to find your way ahead, and you don't know what you are looking for, which was our situation, it will take longer. But what took us seven years might take someone else a month, or seven months. Nevertheless, the values of 'community' and 'sonship' have to be taught.

What we love, cling to and serve, will come out of what we believe. So in order for believers to have a heart for something, they need to be given compelling information, and taught a Biblical understanding of love and relationships.

In seeking to establish 'community' amongst believers, we teach such heart values as would cause believers to at least want to love other believers, and want to see these believers love one another. We teach honour toward leaders, and the desirability of really being 'a people.' What is then needed is for God to place upon those values the power of His grace.

The Values of 'Sonship' and of Christian Community

In aspiring to this elusive thing called 'community,' the spirit of 'sonship' is a big part of the answer – because it deals so purely, and so Biblically, with the attitudes and values of the heart – and these are those which are completely and beautifully shown to us in Jesus Christ. This is why Paul uses the attitudes of Christ as our model in Philippians 2. Sonship is an *attitude* of heart, a value system, just as submission itself is also primarily an attitude of heart.

Regarding submission, may I say this is a major message in the Scriptures – but many think of it as an ugly word, partly because it has been abused, and partly because of human nature and fear. The good news is that submission, properly understood, is one of the most beautiful experiences, and one of the loveliest states of heart, in all the faith of Jesus Christ. Where people are found to be built together in humility and submission, Christ is present. This is a precious thing, going beyond the experience of most of us, because we were not brought up in congregations that had any real experience of community.

As I have said elsewhere, the "spirit of sonship" is an apostolic grace which brings about the spiritual maturity of the believer, the revival of apostolic Christianity, and ultimately, the maturity of the church in preparation for the coming of Christ. The values and heart attitudes of the 'spirit of sonship' is the very nature and essence of authentic, apostolic, New Testament Christianity. But to more fully understand 'sonship,' which I have said in my introduction to this book, is the other half of this revelation of grace, you will find many foundational truths laid out in my previous book, *The Spirit of Sonship*.

Just below, I have listed some of what I regard as the heart values of sonship, as might be found in apostolic, Christian community. This is not a list of rules. It is not a set of laws. These should be read simply as beliefs of the heart, attitudes held because of the values of love, as felt by someone enjoying trusting relationships that bless. These should never be upheld as demands upon believers, but the principles of life in them should be sought out, and taught for the understanding of healthy, community, Christian values.

I wrote these, and shared them with my people three years ago, because these are my values – this is what I believe, this is how I live, and these represent the values I teach. As a 'son' in the ministry, and as one in a community of the love of Christ, I outline some of my own values:

- I am not here for myself, or just to please myself or my family. We do not live for ourselves alone; we are here to serve others.

- I am, from the heart, a part of another person's ministry.

- I have a heart of submission towards, and I choose to be accountable to, someone over me in the Lord – a spiritual leader, a father in Christ.

- I see myself as a son to a spiritual father, whether raised by him in the Lord, or "adopted" into such a spiritual family relationship.

- I am free to leave, but I choose love and faithfulness in relationships.

- I am loved by those over me, and they have given me their hearts.

- I have also given my heart to them. I love, and I am loved and accepted.

- I believe I will be more fruitful in ministry and in the Kingdom of God by walking together in love and service with others than by pursuing a more independent course.

- I believe that spiritual maturity comes from pursuing and walking in Biblical relationships.

- I believe that walking in relational maturity, i.e. maintaining mature and Godly relationships, is the real proof of spiritual maturity.

- I believe maturity of relationships is the Biblical goal of "maturity" to which the apostles urged the church (Hebrews 6:1, Ephesians 4:13, John 17:23).

- I believe that this goal of *"spiritual maturity through relational maturity"* is the "perfection of the saints" that the Scriptures refer to (Eph 4:13), and is a pre-requisite to be established in the church, in time and on earth, before Christ comes. [*"love covers over a multitude of sins"* (1 Pet 4:8), *"a radiant church, without stain or wrinkle"* (Eph 5:27), *"Then we will no longer be infants, tossed back and forth"* (Eph 4:14)]

- I believe that having the heart of a son towards my leader, and also having a heart of oneness with the believers in the fellowship, is the outworking of the same spiritual grace.

- I believe God has made a covenant with me, called the Covenant of Peace, through the blood of His Son, and this makes me one with my fellow believers, with Christ, and with God in a holy fellowship. (Isaiah 54:10, Matt 26:28,1 John 1:3)

- I do not make additional covenants or swear vows in an attempt to be more spiritual, or more closely related to other believers, for I am already subject to the Covenant of Peace, and all its provisions and graces are available to me through the way of Christ alone. (Matt 5:34-37, James 5:12)

- I am in Christ, and therefore I am already in covenant relationship with my leaders, and my believing brothers and sisters.
- I am compelled by the love of God to love my brethren, to see myself as one with them, to honour, love, and serve them, and the requirement to love is a continuing debt I owe my brethren. (Romans 13:8)
- I must guard my heart so that my love never grows cold toward my brethren and my leaders.
- I choose to learn and grow in this matter of loving, honouring, serving, and learning from leaders and spiritual fathers, and in continuing to love, serve, accept, and honour other believers.

And following are a few more generic values for members of a community:

- I need to be praying, working for, and supporting the corporate apostolic mission of my people.

- I believe the God-given corporate goals of the fellowship, the community of believers, are my goals too, and normally they are equally important with anything I feel the Lord tells me personally to do.

- I believe I must not neglect meeting with the believers, and fully participating in the fellowship and prayers of the saints.

- My finance should be devoted to God's service, and not just to my own or my family's earthly gain.

- I believe the Spirit of Grace guides in what to spend, save, or invest, and in what to give or sow; I must listen to the Lord so as to be a fruitful, obedient servant to Christ, to our leaders, and to my brethren.

Remember, these are not vows. They are simply the things I believe. They are values of the heart out of which I live, for Christ's sake. In the next chapter, you will see why they are not, and must never be vows, but are powerful as the resolution of the heart of love.

CHAPTER-NINE

THE DANGER *Of Vows* AND COVENANTS

But I tell you, Do not swear at all...
Simply let your 'Yes' be "Yes,' and your 'No,' 'No;'
anything beyond this comes from the evil one."
Matthew 5: 33, 37

How do you maintain a revival once you have one? The question is relevant, because most of the revivals in history have been very short-lived. Not many revivals last more than a year or two; some last only a day or two. Who wants to go through years of prayer to obtain something from the Lord only to have it dissipate?

I will come to the specific issue of vows and covenants in a moment, but first some background is needed. Years ago

I spent time seeking the Lord on this important question – because my heart's desire was to see a revival that would span multiple generations.

One of the conclusions I came to is that revival fades and disappears off the scene because of what its leaders do, rather than because of what God does.

Another conclusion I came to was this: We maintain a revival the same way we obtain a revival. A revival is given by grace, and needs to stay in the way of grace – but this is often departed from once a revival has been established. Therefore, we must conclude, the spiritual means that had to be in place to obtain it, must remain in place to maintain it.

The way we usually go about looking to God for revival is by passionately and importunately seeking God, and we move more towards revival as we create a dependence on God, and believe. Being totally dependent on God is a big factor in obtaining revival. We do a lot of praying and believing, and listening and waiting, until we come to the place where we do not trust ourselves – neither do we attempt to control God's people, or hinder or control what God wants to do. These are all important elements in obtaining the revival. They then become important elements in keeping it.

When praying and asking the Lord for answers to the question, I felt led to a book I had, but have since lost (through lending I think), by Jonathan Edwards on revival, and found in it some things that really surprised and shocked me. Jonathan Edwards was a truly great man, highly respected by John Wesley, and considered to be the father of the Great Spiritual Awakening, a revival which took place in the 1730s and 1740s.

Three of his articles were published in this one book. One is called *A Narrative of Surprising Conversions*, another *The Distinguishing Marks of a Work of the Spirit of God,* and the third, *An Account of the Revival of Religion in Northampton in 1742.*[1] The articles have amazing stories of things God had done among them, including examples of what today we call manifestations of the Spirit. It needed great theologians like Jonathan Edwards to defend in his day what God was doing, because there were many who said it was the devil.

Edwards had a great heart and very ordered mind, and he observed and understand many things to do with grace, and sin, and human nature, and society life, etc. In these articles is to be found a great deal that is very heart-moving. However, there are also accounts of things that happened where no relationship of cause and effect is observed. It is possible for us to look at these accounts and see some cause and effect at work beyond Edward's observations, but bear in mind, we have had 300 years more experience to aid us.

There are wonderful stories of how the Spirit of God fell on people and changed them completely, often transforming whole towns and communities. The presence of God was all encompassing, and people wanted to sort out their salvation and seek God, and to worship and pray. Communities in which there had been immorality and drunkenness became filled with light and rejoicing.

After recounting these stories, he conveyed the following:

> *About the same time there were two remarkable instances of persons led away with strange enthusiastic delusions.*

'Enthusiasm' was a word used to describe the motive of

1 These articles are public domain, and can be found on the internet.

people who were considered 'flaky', 'super spiritual' as we would say, or 'over the top'. These were people very eager about religion but assumed to be running in the way of the flesh rather than the way of the Spirit. So when we read the word 'enthusiasm' in some of these old writings, it is referring to a spirituality driven by the flesh. This is what they thought about the two mentioned here. What exactly was their fault?

> *That which has made the greatest noise in the country was the conduct of the man at South Hadley. His delusion was that he thought himself divinely instructed to direct a poor man in depression and despairing circumstances to say certain words in prayer to God as recorded in Psalm 116:4 for his own relief.*

In modern English, this was a brother who thought the Lord had impressed on him to tell another brother, one who was really struggling, to pray according to Ps 116: 4, and God would help him. Ps 116: 4 says, *"Lord save me."* The "strange enthusiastic delusion" referred to was simply that an ordinary member of the congregation thought he heard from God that he should give a word of encouragement to a brother.

If this leaves you shaking your head, remember we are living in different times. Can you see how far the church has come? Edwards goes on:

> *The man is esteemed a pious man* (in other words, he is a godly Christian). *I have seen this error of his, had a particular acquaintance with him and I believe that none would question his piety who had known him. And he gave me a particular account of the manner of how he was deluded which is too long to be here inserted. But in short,*

he had exceedingly rejoiced and was elevated in his heart (in other words he was very joyful) *with the extraordinary work of God that was being carried on in the country and came to hold an opinion that it was the beginning of the glorious times of the church spoken of in Scripture. He read it as the opinion of some theologians that many in these times would be endued with extraordinary gifts of the Holy Spirit and he embraced that idea, although previously he had no false apprehensions that anyone except a minister would have such gifts.*

The man's 'delusion' was, having read that in the last times the Holy Spirit would give gifts to all believers and not just to ministers, he thought, because of the revival, the time must have come, and so hc believed God. However, his leaders thought it was delusion. The finale is this:

He exceedingly laments the dishonour he has done to God and the wound he has given religion and has laid low before God and man for it.

In other words, he humbled himself and repented from thinking he could be used by the Holy Spirit.

In Edward's day they seem to have believed two falsehoods. One, that only some people were ministers, and the other, that only those few people who were ministers could be led by the Spirit to give other people help in finding God. Today, we would see these as serious, unbiblical errors. We should thank God that we live with today's light and correspondingly greater freedom.

Edward's narrative said there were two people who had these delusions. It seemed to me that these were two witnesses pointing to where the Spirit of God wanted to take that revival, but it was not to be. This occurred in the year

1742, and that year saw the end of the revival.

The Great Awakening had two main periods, 1735-6, and then the height of the revival occurring from 1740-42. After Jonathan Edwards finished recounting the details of the 'deluded' man, he goes on, and without drawing any connections between events, he made this statement:

After these things, the instances of conversion were rare.

It seems it was all over. He further summarises:

The Spirit of God not long after this, appeared to be withdrawing from all parts of the country.

If we wish to maintain revival, or wish to remain in grace, here is the first error to be avoided – the error of resisting what God wants to do. There has never yet been a revival where God hasn't sought to 'push back the envelope' (boundaries that are in our minds, not His), and of course the Lord will do it again.

In many of the great revivals, the Spirit of God did things that many of the established Christians declared to be the devil. If we remain locked into a traditional mindset of church life, we will be blind to much in the Scriptures. Jesus told the religious leaders of His day, "*...you nullify the word of God for the sake of your tradition.*" (Matthew 15: 6) We have to be very careful about our traditions and cultural assumptions, which often cause us to not see, or not believe, what God has for us, even when the Scriptures plainly offer it.

A couple of days later, still seeking the Lord for answers to my question, I picked up the book again, and read the third article by Jonathan Edward's, *An Account of the Revival of Religion in Northampton in 1742.* Edwards tells of a most powerful time in the revival, the Spring of 1742. The revival was at its height, the whole town had been changed, and many were by this time converted. The town was alive with the presence and power of God by night and day. All night long all over town lights were burning, with people up worshipping, singing, and praying. He wrote the following about events in February, 1742:

> *... the people were exceedingly moved crying out in great numbers in the meeting house, and a great part of the congregation commonly staying in the house of God for hours after the public service. Many also were exceedingly moved in private meetings...* almost *the whole town seemed to be in a great and continual commotion, day and night, and there was indeed a very great revival of religion...*
>
> *When I came home, I found the town in very extraordinary circumstances, such as, in some respects, I never saw it in before...*
>
> *...and there were some instances of persons lying in a sort of trance, remaining perhaps for a whole 24 hours motionless, and with their senses locked up; but in the meantime under strong imaginations, as though they went to heaven and had there a vision of glorious and delightful objects.*

Edwards was so grateful to God for the revival that had transformed his people. God had blessed them so much in it that they must keep it at all costs. What were they to do to keep the people in revival?

He believed that to keep the revival, and to consolidate the work God had done, the people needed to enter into a solemn oath and covenant before God. In March, 1742, he drew up such a document, which is recorded in full and took up four pages of the book. He first proposed it to key leaders, then to various groups in the church, then publically to the church, and put copies in the hands of the deacons, so that anyone in the church could read it. After that, he had everyone over 14 years of age subscribe to it by a show of hands, and then a special day for prayer and fasting was set aside, 16th March, 1742, when everyone came before God to consecrate themselves in this solemn vow together. Thus He wrote:

> *...I led the people into a solemn public renewal of their covenant with God.*

That covenant specified a great deal about the way Christians should live – and the kind of things we believe too. But what it did was to lock-up the way Christians should live and respond to God into a legalistic structure. In drawing up such a document, and having the people make a vow to God, with a long list of things they promised that they would and wouldn't do, including the way they would treat other people, the way they would be honest in business, and the way in which they would keep themselves fervent in prayer, and attending to the call of God, only succeeded in putting on the people a legalistic obligation.

Yet this was contrary to the spirit of what had happened to them in the Awakening. The Spirit of God had come to town in answer to prayer, and had taken hold of all the people who had been lukewarm and backslidden, and the many unconverted, and taken hold of the faithful Christians as well, and brought them all into a tremendous relationship with God where they were full of love and on fire for God. They had become exactly the way you would want them to be. And then man, well-intentioned though he was, decided to keep the people the way they needed to be by making them take a very extensive, exhaustive, joyless set of vows that were supposedly the answer to them maintaining love and joy. But love and joy never come from vows, and joy is usually the first thing to depart when the law comes in, as does freedom.

In this covenant there was much said to the effect that they recognised that loving and serving God so fully would not be natural to them, and their hearts would want to get away from it, so they were asking God to obligate them to it. When you come to the end of the document, he has them promising:

> *"...to be often strictly examining ourselves by these promises..."*

And then has them asking God,

> *...for Christ's sake, keep us from wickedly dissembling these, our solemn vows;*

In other words, keep our wicked hearts from trying to avoid these vows, and then he includes the oath with these words:

> *"...that He who searches our hearts, and ponders the path of our feet, would, from time to time, help us in trying ourselves by this covenant..."*

Of course, you could read every statement in that document and agree that this is how we should live, and it would be great if we all did. But only grace can change lives and behaviour and bring in love, joy, freedom, passion, worship, and hunger for God as a permanent state of the heart. No form of law can ever achieve this, otherwise God would never have needed to say what He said in Jeremiah 31: 31, and neither would we ever need the cross or a Saviour.

However, Edwards, with the accepted values of his time and the culture of his religious background, and having drawn up a lengthy document, met with all the people to make a legalistic vow as a covenant with God in the hope that this would maintain the revival, when in fact, this was the very thing that killed it, as we shall see.

After the recording of the vow in his *Account*, a double paragraph break occurs to begin a new section. It does not appear that he himself consciously connected what he had just written with what follows, but his next statement, written immediately after the vow, is this:

> *In the beginning of the summer of 1742, there seemed to be an abatement of the liveliness of people's affection in religion...*

This was perhaps some 10 weeks afterwards, yet the revival had immediately waned, and come to an end, and what he tells is a very sad tale. He went on to say:

> *...in general, people's engagedness in religion, and the liveliness of their affections have been on the decline; and some of the young people especially have shamefully lost their liveliness and vigour in religion, and much of the seriousness and solemnity of their spirits.*

It was the youth, and the younger adults and their children, who had specially been revived, many of whom now drifted back to old ways. He assured us that many also remained as solid, eminent Christians, as we would expect. But the revival was over, and all the power in soul-saving was gone. The making of that Solemn Oath and Covenant, along with all its vows, was the direct and immediate cause of the ending of the Great Awakening.

In this chapter I have brought up two different kinds

of events that occurred in the Great Awakening. Each of these kinds of things does something to change the faith of the people. They remove the freedom of Christ, empty the heart, and take away the hunger.

The first error was to declare, about something God was trying to do, that it was foolish man and not God. In calling the Spirit flesh, they were quenching the Spirit.

The second mistake was to recognise something that God was doing, but try to keep it and control it, or improve it, by fleshly means. This is an attempt to use the strength of the flesh to maintain the work of the Spirit. Both these dangers we must avoid.

You cannot take a system of law and impose it on revival to create some kind of spiritual order. It has to be a work of grace. We all need to find a greater grace from God than we do have, and we will only maintain what we have by walking in the way of grace.

Consider the effect of these two events. In the first case, the whole church in the whole country hears of these so-called delusions that get squashed by the leaders of the church. All the other believers are then frightened to move. Impressed on their minds all the more is that they cannot hear God for themselves, they have to rely on the minister. That has the effect of forcing them into a mould that locks them in. This takes away faith, freedom, and hunger, all three. If the revival at that point begins to fall off, it is not falling off because God is leaving; it is falling off because the people who were hungry are no longer hungry. The people who were enjoying freedom no longer think they have freedom. The people who had faith for God now have a lesser faith.

We find the same with the other story. This whole town of believers, who had been wonderfully enjoying God and the freedom that faith and grace had given, then stood up and took a vow to bind themselves by law and obligation to these things. Now they must try to maintain their revived hearts by following through with all the vows they made, but it is not possible, because the law removed the power, not to mention the joy which always leaves when the law comes in.

Vows and human covenants always take away freedom, and kill off faith and hunger for God. It is no wonder that the very next thing that Edwards describes in his *Account*, after outlining the Solemn Oath and Covenant, was that all the love and faith of the church seemed to have gone.

That is why I said earlier that the ongoing course of revival is more determined by what people do with it, than by what God does. Everything that God wants to do with us is by grace alone, and we have to be very careful not to lock ourselves into a legalistic Christianity.

When I first made this discovery about the devastating effect of vows and covenants from the tales of the Great Awakening, I was very, very surprised. And shocked! I thought impulsively, "It couldn't be!" All my life, almost 40 years in churches at the time, we had included vows, pledges, covenants, and promises to God, in our service to Christ. My first reactive thought was, "Surely we are supposed to make promises and covenants in Christian service."

I felt that way because I had been raised in The Salvation Army, and our lives were full of that kind of thing. From the Junior Soldier's Pledge, in which you publically make brief, simple promises, to the Senior Soldier's "Articles of War," which is a really long document in fine print, in which you promise everything 'holy' imaginable about the way you will live and serve, and pledge to be faithful to the principles of the Salvation Army until you die. Not only that, when we became Salvation Army Officers, as we did at the end of 1975, there was a day called Covenant Day, as there always is for cadets about to be commissioned. This is the day devoted to worship and prayer in which, every one of you, at some point of personal surrender and final commitment, is to go forward and kneel and sign a covenant with God.

Whilst that covenant is only an attempt to help people feel devoted, and therefore more likely to be faithful to the ministry of Jesus Christ, statistically, the majority of people who sign that covenant do not last in the ministry. Certainly the 'survival rates' are no better for this than what other religious institutions might do. We were told in the college that, on average, more than half of us would leave the ministry within 10 years – this was in the context of exhorting us, quite properly, to guard our hearts.

But you can see why, with this background, I was incredulous at the thought that these things might be totally alien to spiritual victory in the New Covenant. There was only one thing to do. I immediately went to the Scriptures to search, not the Old Testament but the New, for the place of vows and covenants. And I was surprised again, for I discovered that they are non-existent.

I looked up all the associated words I could think of in the translation I was using for the purpose – "promise," "promises," promised," (because we always think we should make promises to God), and "vow," "pledge," "covenant," etc. What did I find? There are dozens of references to promises in the New Testament, and every single one of them is about promises that God makes to us. There was not a single verse I could find in the New Testament about us being asked to, or needing to, make promises to God.

Searching on the word ***covenant*** reveals that this word is used exclusively in the New Testament to discuss what *God* has said or done concerning us. There is no example of anyone in the New Testament making a covenant with God. It is always a case of God making covenant with us through the blood of His Son. And there is a Scripture that ought to make us pause with great caution: *"Just as no one can set aside or add to a human covenant that has been duly established..."* (Galatians 3: 15) This shows the very ongoing, binding nature of covenants.

For the word ***vow*** I found a few references. They generally have to do with Jewish Christians who were keeping Jewish customs. And in Paul's case, it was supposed to help him stay out of trouble in Jerusalem by looking like a zealous Jew, but all it did was get him into worse trouble.

The more obvious example is that of the many widows in the early church who, with the loss of their husbands, had been left without means. Many of them were very needy, and the church did much to help them. We find a Biblical reference (1 Timothy 5:11-12) to a custom in the early church where some widows would apparently pledge to live the rest of their lives for the purpose of service to the saints and the church. Thus they had a sense of purpose, a helpful connection to being supported by the love of the church, but were to live exemplary and separated lives. Some of these in earlier times were apparently still young or at least of very active years, for Paul comments that some of them, after making a commitment to devote their lives for the service of Christ and the church, had married again, and given the enemy an opportunity for reproach upon the church. This had, apparently, much to do with the culture of the day in which they lived.

Paul was alarmed for the spiritual consequences of this, since making vows and then ignoring them would bring these women under condemnation, and they had failed to keep the first vow when they made a second one, the marriage vow. His advice to younger widows was to stay free of vows so as to get married and have children if there was the opportunity, without risking the condemnation of broken vows. Paul's words at this point arc not exactly a prohibition, but certainly reveal that people play with grave dangers when getting involved with vows.

If you make a vow to God, you are meant to keep it. Being a God of grace, He won't let you just break a vow, but He will allow you to repent of a vow, and find in Him a release from it. That is different.

As I looked back on the course of my life I realised that just about every vow I ever made I have had to repent of, and be released from. There may be a place for vows, and perhaps sometimes God will call someone to a vow, but you had better be sure that it is of the Spirit – yet our tendency is to do these things in the flesh, out of a religious nature that takes pride in the flesh. There are huge dangers. Fortunately there is the grace and beauty of repentance, and with the Lord there is forgiveness of sins (Colossians 1:14). Unfortunately, our foolishness has often cost us much by the time we get ourselves free from things the Lord never put upon us.

A Truly Great Pledge

The NIV translation uses the English word pledge in the apostle Peter's teaching about the meaning of baptism (1 Peter 3: 21), but this is not a pledge in the sense of making a vow, and other translations do not use this word. Rather than the NIV's *"...the pledge of a good conscience toward God,"* the NASB has *"an appeal to God for a good conscience...,"* and the KJV has *"...the answer of a good conscience toward God."* The NIV footnote has the alternative word as "response," in keeping with the meaning of the Greek term used by Peter. What could Peter's statement mean for us.

The word 'response' and 'answer' will help us here, and the word 'pledge' is also useful, for this all refers surely to something we have given to God.

Baptism is the only 'pledge' you will ever need – it is the only real, wonderful, workable, and God-given one, and is the one which does remove all need for any other. Baptism is that occasion when, as a result of repentance and faith, you surrender all to Christ, and in obedience submit to baptism, believing that you no longer live but Christ lives in you, and that you are dead to the world, having been crucified with Christ, and the world crucified to you. In all good conscience, you are saying to God that you are giving everything you are, and everything you have, to Him. Your heart has been surrendered, and you are now completely His. As far as you know, you have handed yourself over. This is your 'answer,' and it is a real pledge. It is then up to the Holy Spirit to work with what you have given Him – to refine and sanctify you. So if your motives are not completely pure, it is His job to help you get them pure.

That, baptism, is a pledge we should make. It is a declaration that, from this point on, your whole life is the Lord's. Baptism is our appropriate response to the claims of Christ. But that is the last pledge you should ever make because, properly, you have handed everything over. You now are to live by the light of His Word and the help of the Holy Spirit. But if you start making vows, like, "I will rise at 3 a.m. everyday for the rest of my life for prayer," or "I will read a minimum of five chapters of the Bible every day," you are setting yourself up for failure.

But Resolve is Good

Please note: all this about the deadly danger of vows does not mean there is not a place for *resolve*. Resolution (the resolve of our hearts) is what Jesus was referring to in Matthew 5:37 when He said, *"Simply let your 'Yes' be "Yes,' and your 'No,' 'No;'"* Resolution to act, goal setting, aims and purpose, good decisions, and commitments are all part of a healthy life in your obedient service of Christ. We should not be frightened to make decisions or commitments, led by the Spirit, and in doing so, always keep our word. But see that Jesus added here, *"...anything beyond this comes from the evil one."*

Now examine more fully what Jesus said about vows in the Sermon on the Mount, where He is obviously making a complete distinction between practices under the Old Covenant and the New. I think His instruction is very clear, and we should be surprised that we have been so slow to see that it applies to the death-dealing practices so many of us have engaged in, in making covenants and vows – and this has occurred in every branch of the church historically.

Jesus speaks:

> *"Again, you have heard that it was said to the people long ago, 'Do not break your oath, but keep the oaths you have made to the Lord.' But I tell you, Do not swear at all...*
> *Simply let your 'Yes' be "Yes,' and your 'No,' 'No;' anything beyond this comes from the evil one." (Matthew 5: 33, 37)*

What about Marriage Vows?

Some will want to know how this affects marriage vows. So more as an aside, may I say, there are two things we need to understand.

Firstly, marriage is a covenant designed and instituted by God, not man. Therefore it is a blessing, and a grace. As such, it fits in well with what we have already discussed. I said earlier that in New Testament Christianity, all legitimate covenants are given by God to man, and we should not enter into covenants of our own private making. When a man and a woman enter marriage, they enter into a relationship of grace that has been designed for mankind since the creation, and its meaning and terms have been set by the same sovereign Creator who had the blood of His Son in mind for us, and who instituted the marriage covenant as a picture in the earth of the intimate relationship that is Christ and the church. This is why marriage is holy.

The second thing we need to understand is that the security or health or longevity of a marriage is not so much determined by the vows a couple make, as it is by the relationship they have, and what is in their hearts. In marriage there is a giving of the heart to each other, which should never be removed, and this is in fact what God designed marriage for. The many marriages which last for life have not necessarily lasted because of the vows, and the many marriages that have failed have not been kept from failing even though they had taken vows. This is why I think it is true to say that marriages that stay together are held together not by vows, but by what is in the hearts of the individuals. And generally, that will be not only love and faithfulness, but a deep knowledge and sense, on some inner bedrock of the heart, that they are one with, and belong to, are in fact *married* to, their partner for life. These are beliefs, or heart knowledge.

I don't know about other nations, but under Australian law no vows as such are required for a legal marriage. For a marriage to be legal, our law requires only that the groom states publicly that he takes the woman to be his wife, the bride states that she takes the groom to be her husband, and for the marriage celebrant to declare them to be married. Anything beyond this, as far as the law is concerned, is rather the important matter of having a suitable ceremony for the marriage to be significant, respected, understood to be intended as permanent, and creating an effective sense of occasion and celebration.

I do not promote the idea that vows in wedding ceremonies should be discarded, because they occupy a rather huge place culturally in both secular and Christian weddings, and help to create that sense of the importance and permanence of marriage. As well, they are usually a reasonably accurate reflection of what the marriage covenant is, and therefore may really help to establish in the heart this inner sense of identity in being one with their spouse for life. But I do not think the glue that actually holds them together in marriage, which is referred to at least four times in Scripture, the first being found in Genesis 2:24, *"For this reason a man will leave his father and mother and be united with his wife, and they will become one flesh,"* comes from any power that vows have, but rather from the Lord who joins them together. And that glue is real, which is why it is so painful when couples separate.

But I do think it would probably be more effective and powerful, and may have a greater effect on the intimacy of the relationship than we realise, if instead of a couple making public declarations in the form of *vows*, they rather made these declarations in the form of *beliefs* they hold. This could include what they believe about marriage, about what God has instituted marriage for, what they believe about giving themselves to each other, about life, about love, about God, about family, etc. We all live out of our values, and act in accordance with what we deeply believe. Vows as vows have no *power* to guide, control, or enhance behaviour in the medium to long term, except to the degree that they are an actual reflection of what we genuinely believe. The challenge then, in marriage preparation, is to establish deeply held beliefs as values. But we do need to be careful in thinking through all the implications, since we are dealing with major issues of life and the well-being of society.

About Financial Commitments: As an aside, I need to explain at this point that when I speak about pledges, I am *not* talking about the use of 'pledges' in the making of fixed term financial commitments to the Lord or a church or ministry. That is not part of this discussion, because it is not the same thing. Where there is a fundraising campaign, and we commit or 'pledge' to give so much a week or month for so long, that is different – that is an exercise in resolve, a decision made to give in a spirit of sacrifice, and these are always non-binding and flexible, in any case. Certainly we should not set these up as a vow, and even though they are often called 'pledges,' in reality it is simply a considered decision to make a financial commitment. Commitments to regular giving are usually holy, and on that subject we are on completely different ground. We usually see believers and churches come into victories because of financial decisions, which, as Jesus made clear, deal with the heart.

Vows and covenants, however, are usually entered into with a different purpose in view – that of increasing righteousness, or spiritual performance. But these things can never be achieved except by grace and the work of the Spirit. Where law is used it will work against the end being sought, and eventually bring in failure and condemnation.

The nature of a vow is that it can never give you power to keep it, but when you fail it produces condemnation, and when you break it, it produces a curse. God never intended this. If you try this, you are trying to improve your Christianity with a bit of law, whereas the Lord wants you to learn to walk with Christ in the freedom of the Holy Spirit, being led by the Spirit day by day. The New Testament teaches the principle that the only way to not break the law is to have no law. You will find that idea in the book of Romans. Victory by grace through freedom is the place to which the Spirit of God wants to bring us –a place to which rules can never bring us. But the covenant made in 1742 refers again and again to living by Christian rules. In the matter of their families, for example, "we will keep the Christian rules."

I was told a story in recent years that is so typical of what happens when Christians make covenants designed to protect relationships. A church in the United States had a group of younger women, some single and some married, that was great at creative ministries – dance, drama, and the like. Not only was what they did in ministry beautiful and effective, but their relationships were so rich. They worked together, loved each other, and co-operated as a team really committed to each other. It was apparently a wonderful thing, and a really sweet thing in the heart of that church. They got to thinking about how great it was to have these rich relationships, and thought they should do something to make sure they keep it all going, so as to not lose what they had. They agreed to make a covenant with each other. Taking an oath, each member promised to walk faithfully in covenant relationship with the others, to continue to love each other in a certain way, and to always do this and never do that, etc, and be committed to the ministry they shared, and be committed to one another – and they all signed it. And, of course, it wasn't long until it all started to come apart. The group didn't last. Dear reader, this will happen every time. It is just so contrary to grace, and so contrary to the New Testament. Oil and water do not mix, and neither do law and grace. We only ever build better and more permanently with grace. Grace is what this group must have had before they reverted to law. The Great Awakening was in grace before they made a covenant.

What, Then, Are We to Believe about Covenants?

I discovered by experience, as I shall explain soon, that even though 'covenant' is a Biblical word, there is danger in its misapplication. After receiving light on this from the Lord, we stopped using the term 'covenant' in our church except in relation to the Covenant that God has made with us all in the blood of His Son.

God has indeed made a covenant with us. That means I have an existing covenant relationship with God, in which He Himself has set the terms – and because I am in covenant relationship with God, I am not to turn around and make my own covenant with God. He has already made the covenant, and the nature of God is that He is a covenant-making, covenant-keeping God. My task is to understand what this covenant is, and to submit to it, and to believe and receive the grace that is in it. It is not for me to make promises to God about how I am going to live – it is for me to understand His commands, and by the power of the Spirit and His grace, obey them.

I also have an existing covenant relationship with other people. God has made a covenant with others, and brought others into covenant with Himself, just as He did me. Therefore, it so happens that this covenant God has made with us each has put us in a relationship with one another, which relationship God has already defined in the one and only covenant.

We are not to turn around and draw up some other covenant. We are not to enter into a so-called covenant relationship on the basis that we need to make some promises to each other. When people do this, misunderstanding the New Covenant they already have, they spoil everything.

We are, therefore, in covenant relationship with others, but never because we have taken vows or made oaths. We simply belong, because of what has been done for us in the blood of the Son of Man, and because God has chosen us for it. If we properly understand this covenant that God has made with us, we belong to each other already. We are then to find the grace that already exists in that covenant, and embrace the kind of heart we should have for each other.

These obsolete things such as vows and oaths have no power to bless, but plenty of power to curse. We are not to use them and then call them by this Biblical and spiritual word 'covenant.' It is a Biblical word, but putting a holy, Biblical word onto something illegitimate does not make it holy, or useful.

How would it be if a husband came back from the honeymoon and drew up a list of rules with respect to how the marriage covenant is going to work with him and his wife? Then he posts it in the house, and draws her attention to it. This is how she is now going to live to keep them both happy, she is told. They are not both going to be happy for very long if he does that. It just doesn't work like this. Neither is this the way God does things with us.

If in ministry I was to have a formal covenant relationship with my apostolic leader and spiritual father, and we "signed off" on it and took a vow about being committed, and promised what we would do for each other, all we will have done is to curse the relationship. It won't work very well, it brings in a sense of drudgery, and it won't last as a great relationship. But there are people who get excited about this kind of thing because they think it makes them more spiritual than they were, or more spiritual than others. False joy will carry them on for a while, until it starts turning sour, and eventually goes belly up.

I knew of a fellow in Australia, a young man with a strong ministry gift, but he had fallen on difficult times and wasn't doing that well. A mature minister helped him, and they started walking in a really meaningful relationship. So this young man took an oath, and entering into a vow, pledged himself to remain faithful to this older man as his spiritual father, to walk with him and serve him until he died. It didn't last but a few years, and with the relationship hindered and cursed by law and expectations, it was the one who made the vow who broke it off and walked away frustrated and disappointed. I had told him this kind of thing is a curse and ought to be rescinded before it was too late. Had he set aside the vow, and gone back to relationship of the heart, that may well have saved the situation.

A great error is made when we make vows or covenants, because when we do, we have decided to live by our own words, instead of by God's Word. It's as if wc think there are not enough words in the Bible to live by, so we need to make up a few more sentences and paragraphs, and then live by those instead. We fall under the condemnation of the law where there was no law, and we are living by grace no longer. This is pretty serious stuff.

God has given us success in building the lives of people together, to the point where our people love each other and hearts are knit together. Let me say, there is not a vow or an oath amongst anything we do. We are committed to one another, and walk together devotedly, with a great sense of just belonging to each other, but there is no such thing as a promise in the house. Except, of course, for the promises that God has Himself given to us.

Banning the 'Personal' Use of the Word, 'Covenant'

Now you can see the dangers with the use of the word 'covenant.' There is of course an appropriate and Biblical use of it, but I decided that for myself and our church we would simply not use this word except when referring to the covenant God made with us in the blood of His Son. This decision came after five years in which I and the other pastors endeavoured constantly to teach covenant relationship, faithfulness, devotion to one another, and love of the brethren. We taught this repeatedly, with a free use made of the word 'covenant' to describe the relationships we desired our people to find, but without results as I explained earlier in this book.

I came to the place where I could see clearly that the way we were making use of the word itself was a big part of the problem. We had a number of problems with the use of the word 'covenant.' We had a cultural problem, a linguistic problem, and a theological problem, at least. We wanted the relationship, but there had to be another way of describing it in our culture, because this word in Australian culture only made matters worse. We had a linguistic problem simply because people did not understand the word. It is not a word in common usage in the language of today. And aside from the Biblical doctrine of its misuse which we have already covered, there were other reasons also which led to placing a useful and appropriate "ban" on the use of the word in our church. We simply choose to not use the word at all, except, as I said, in its prime use, to speak of the covenant that God has made with us in the blood of His Son.

And the result? We have found success and freedom in relationships to a degree that many only dream of, which developed soon after getting rid of the sloppy, culturally legalistic, demanding, and unbiblical, use of the word. The wrong use of the word is very threatening, especially to men in Australian culture, yet at the same time, using a different vocabulary, the relationships we seek to develop are a deeply ingrained value in Australian culture, especially for men. The difference? Our old-fashioned obsolete church use of the word 'covenant' portrayed the legal obligations of a binding religiosity that was foreign and threatening – but Australian cultural and everyday terms were more in keeping with love and heart relationships, that did not threaten but warmed hearts. And as well, we were without the curse of the law.

A Call to First Love

The New Testament does not call us to keep rules, or to make vows and pledges. But there is one thing the Bible does call us back to – our first love. This we shall take a brief look at next, including the way it brings our hearts to the obedience to Christ and the Holy Spirit which has replaced the law – the love that has made distracting and harmful vows and covenants completely obsolete.

CHAPTER-TEN

The Recall to *First Love*

"You have forsaken your first love.
Remember the height from which you have fallen!
Repent and do the things you did at first."
Revelation 2:4b-5a

The New Testament doesn't call us to make vows and pledges. But there is one thing the Bible does call us back to – our first love, which is Jesus and His people. In the book of Revelation, in Christ's letter to the Ephesian church, He said there was nothing wrong with their work. As far as their service to Christ was concerned, you would have thought they measured up. *"I know your deeds, your hard work and your perseverance. I know that you cannot tolerate wicked men, that you have tested those who claim to be apostles but are not, and have found them false. You have persevered and have endured hardships for my name, and have not grown weary.*" You would think this was a fantastic church. Outwardly, they really measured up. But the Lord Jesus continued, "*Yet I hold this against you: You have forsaken your first love.*" (Revelation 2: 2-3, 4)

Dear friends, Christ never intended that we would walk by laws, but He did intend that we would walk in love. A verse of an old Salvation Army song asked, "H*ave I worked for hireling wages, or as one with vows to keep?*" The song is titled "All my work is for the Master". We used to sing this often, and a very moving song it was too. I have thought more about these words in recent times. The songwriter was right enough in pointing out there are two different motives of the heart in serving God, and some people do fall into the category of the hireling.

Or do I serve 'as one with vows to keep?' continued the song. There we have a problem. If we measure ourselves by vows and rules, it makes it harder for us, not easier, and allows less room for the Spirit of God to do what He wants to do in us. It would be more accurate to ask, "Have I worked for hireling wages, or as one motivated by love?'

Unless we can come to God without fear and without rules, but knowing that He accepts and loves us completely, and we come because we ourselves love also, we will not be able to ever give to God what He is looking for. Even if you kept all the rules, this would not give to God what He is looking for in you.

God is looking for something that cannot be produced by rules, which is why in the new covenant God has Himself dealt with the demands of the law. God is looking for intimacy. He is looking to know and love you intimately, and for you to know and love Him intimately. If ever a relationship is based on rules, you will not find intimacy, because in such a relationship there is always pressure and demand for performance. The need to measure up removes trust, and law always produces failure in the measuring-up department. If the relationship is based on love you can succeed, because it is based on acceptance, approval, and longing for one another, causing intimacy and trust to grow.

In marriage, if a husband says to his wife, "Unless the toast every morning is exactly the right shade of brown, I can never love you," that would be just plain stupidity, especially if he wanted intimacy and trust in relationship with her. But most of us think this is what God does. We think that unless we have kept the rules, we cannot possibly be acceptable to Him.

God is not looking for you and I to be so incredibly perfect that we measure up to our own expectations of what good religion is, for the same reason that husbands and wives will never enter into a deeper intimacy if marriage is based on rules. You can only create intimacy in a relationship if there is complete acceptance, flexibility, and complete forgiveness. Then there is not an issue if something goes wrong. So if you happen to say something wrong or do something wrong, it need not be an issue that spoils intimacy – it can be dealt with by grace. In that environment you can have intimacy.

Now we can see why God doesn't major on the rules. When we let the Spirit of God into our hearts, we will see our own sinful state compared with His holiness. There will be times when that overwhelming sense of how Holy He is, and how Awesome, will come over us. You will go to your knees in repentance, and weep, and cry out to God, and find that it is the most beautiful experience of life you ever had. God reveals Himself in His holiness, and reveals your sin, so that He can actually bring you near.

In C.S. Lewis' Narnia Chronicles, one of the characters came face to face with Aslan the Lion, a representation of Christ. In the face of this lion she was overcome with awe and fear, but it was presented as an awesome thing. She said something to the lion like, "Sir, you are so beautiful, I would rather be eaten by you than fed by anyone else." This is much like what happens when you come into the presence of God, and get a 'glimpse', metaphorically speaking, of something of Him – it is frightening, but in a way that you want to be frightened by Him. And it draws you to His heart and brings you to repentance – and what comes from it is magnificent, wonderful love. But all of this is through relationship, i.e. personal interaction.

After reading Edward's *Account*, and having seen the devastation caused by fleshly covenants and vows, I spent the following Sunday morning teaching our church what I had learned, based on the theme of grace and our need to keep ourselves in the spirit of whatever God might do with us. I taught a strong message against the making of vows and covenants.

But the Lord had more to say. After church, having just got into the car and about to drive home, the Lord spoke: ***"Why do you need to make vows, when you have my commands?"***

That comparison made it obvious – why do we need to write our own words to define how to live, when God has already given us His words about how to live? We are not to live by keeping our own set of rules, but by searching His word for the knowledge of how to walk with Him and please Him. We should never set the value of our words above His word by incorporating ours into vows and covenants.

A few days later, early in the morning when listening to the Lord, He showed me again why we do not need to make vows. He gave me Psalm 119: 32, *"I run in the path of your commands."* You simply do not need vows, because we have His commands. You do not need to make up for yourself new and extra rules, and treat these as if they are 'scripture'. Jesus has already told us how to live. Our emphasis for life should be focused on listening to what God has to say.

This does not mean the people of God can run amuck and do whatever they like. The Lord says to run in the way of His commands, and the Lord is looking for the response of your heart.

Ps 119 is full of precious words. You won't find any better devotional reading than Ps 119. Consider the following portions:

> *You have laid down precepts that are to be fully obeyed.* (v. 4)

> *Oh that my ways were steadfast in obeying your*

> *decrees! Then I would not be put to shame when I consider all your commands.* (v. 5-6)
>
> *I seek you with all my heart; do not let me stray from all your commands.* (v. 10)
>
> *I rejoice in following your statutes as one rejoices in great riches.* (v. 14)
>
> *I meditate on your precepts and consider your ways.* (v. 15)
>
> *Your statutes are my delight; they are my counselors.* (v. 24)
>
> *I run in the path of your commands.* (v. 32)

The full sentence of verse 32 reads, "*I run in the path of your commands, because you have set my heart free.*" That is *gospel* truth. The freedom and liberty is real. Our hearts have been given a freedom to choose right and to choose grace, which is why the Psalmist accurately rejoices in grace when he said the Lord had set his heart free to run in the way of God's commands. It reminds us of Paul's words, "For s*in shall not be your master, because you are not under law, but under grace.*" (Romans 6: 14, but see 12-14)

If you chose today to obey the Lord more perfectly, where would you start? You would start with the commands to *"Love the Lord your God with all your heart and with all your soul and with all your mind,*" and *"Love your neighbour as yourself.*" (Matthew 22:37, 39) The first word here is love. If we were seeking to obey God and run in the path of His commands, we would start here because this is the great commandment, and Jesus indicates that if you obey Him in this, you will have satisfied all His commands. Does it not make sense that we should start with the command He puts first, especially if it wraps up all the others.

But the way human religiosity thinks is vows! Vows will help us obey God! And we fill our vows up with things like getting up at 5 a.m. to pray, or going to the prayer meetings every day (which are really good things to do, but not good as the subject of vows). We put *doing things*, all of which are great when done out of freedom and for the right motive of seeking God, in place of *love as obedience*.

We always tend to put a religious and legalistic structure on things, when what the Lord is looking for is life. The Lord knows that if we listen to what He is saying to us, and obey that, it will bring us life and freedom. But if we create a whole religious system out of it, it brings death instead. We need to forget the legalism and listen to what He is saying.

"If you loved me…" is not Control

Jesus said, *"If you love Me, you will obey what I command."* (John 14: 15) You can, of course, read this statement in different ways. But if you know Jesus, you know to be looking for a meaning that is life-giving.

What happens in our culture every day, with husbands and wives, and engaged and courting couples, is they sometimes use that kind of language – "if you loved me," – and it is easily recognised as control. "If you loved me, you would do this…"

Yet here is Jesus saying the same thing, *"If you love Me…"* He must mean something other than manipulation.

He is not holding out on us. What is the meaning that gives freedom? He is not making demands, rather He is making an observation about how our hearts work. He is saying that it just so happens when you find the way of love, you discover that obedience comes more easily. That is why we have to go back to the love command.

It is also His command that we love others, as for example when He said, *"Love your neighbour as yourself."* This is where perhaps too many are not yet obedient. Now you might have put something in your offering to help someone. You might include others in your prayers. You might have done a lot of things that have made your conscience feel better, but you still haven't loved if you won't change your lifestyle for the sake of another person.

One night we got into deep prayer for the lost of our city, pleading that they would come to Christ. It became very evident to us, when we were in the Spirit, that one of the reasons we do not really see people coming to Christ is that we don't love them. I was pleading with God for children. Remember Rachel, the wife of Jacob, who thought he was marrying her and got Leah instead, and had to serve another seven years for Rachel. Leah started having children, but Rachel had none, so her desperate cry to Jacob was, *"Give me children, or I'll die!"* (Genesis 30:1) God did hear her prayer and open her womb. This also was the cry of our heart on the floor of the prayer room that night: "Give us children, children, children."

One of the things revealed by the Spirit that night was that one of the hindrances to obtaining spiritual children in the church (I am not saying this is a present matter, but was part of the church at some point in time) was that some people had despised their own children. In the past there had been an element of mothers or fathers being exasperated with their children, and angry with the demands their kids made on them, and they had closed their hearts to loving their children more, or having more children, or whatever. The Spirit of God took this up with us. It was a case where, because there had been in the church a heart attitude against the natural children, it cursed the spiritual womb of the church from bearing God's children.

So what about the lost? If you are too comfortable or too busy or too tired to want to help another person, there is something wrong. If you are a follower of Jesus, you are meant to be the Good Samaritan. He was one who would not pass by on the other side of the road, but at the expense of his own time and money he *stopped,* and gave succour to the suffering man, even though the Jews hated the Samaritans.

So today or tomorrow, are you willing to stop on your journey and help another person? If you do that, you are walking in the love of Christ. If you are not doing so, the truth is that you have allowed your heart to be distracted from the purpose of God. Perhaps your love has grown cold, and your heart is not running in the way you were commanded.

His first command, as we said, is to love. How about we forget all the other commands for a while, and try and get this one right. We are meant to love not only Him who loves us, and not only love each other. We are meant to love all whom we meet. If you love them, and are willing to make time for them, God may just give spiritual children.

How can you test your heart to see what your love is like? In the end, at any time in the life of the church, it will come down to this. When a new believer comes in, having just turned to Jesus, are you prepared to take the time to teach them about the ways of Jesus?

We do not live for ourselves – not if we are followers of Christ. We are to live for others. Otherwise, even if a revival were to start, it would not remain. One of the keys to keeping revival alive is, surely, that we must care about the people who are turning to Jesus. If that isn't our first priority, revival will die. His Spirit, for that purpose, will be removed.

When our own values need to change, we need to go to the cross, and then to Pentecost. If we try to change our value systems by ourselves, we are relying on natural strength instead of finding grace. But if we go to the throne of grace, we will obtain mercy and find the power of grace does indeed change us.

In times past, Christians would have obtained a sense of spirituality, of religious identity, and a sense of being in the presence of God from a magnificent building such as a cathedral. It was as though to go into the building was to be in the presence of God.

But in these centuries since the reformation, for many that sense of identity and of being in the will of God came from being in what they thought was the right denomination, with the right doctrine. (Not that their doctrine necessarily called for this, it is more the outcome of man being innately religious and competitive.) But a denomination is another type of building; neither of those forms of 'assurance' is anything like apostolic Christianity.

In real, apostolic, New Testament Christianity, we get our sense of identity from belonging to a fellowship of *people*, whom we love, with whom we are one. I am not here referring to that assurance of salvation and the inner witness which only God the Holy Spirit can give, but to that more general but very important sense we must have of belonging, of being in the will of God, of being 'at home' with God's people, which is also crucial for our sense of identity and well-being – but which only properly comes when we are not independent, but yielded and in submission.

Paul said that we should test ourselves to see whether we are in the faith. (2 Corinthians 13:5) But how are we to test ourselves? Is the test one of believing the right doctrine? No, for doctrine cannot save you.

The Bible test of whether we are in the faith is a simple one. What it comes down to in the end is the question of whether we love the brethren, for loving the brethren whom we can see is the evidence that we have loved Christ.

Here is the Biblical position with regard to the question of how we can test ourselves:

> *"We know that we have passed from death to life, because we love our brothers. Anyone who does not love remains in death."* (1 John 3:14)

So it is not a question of which denomination we belong to, or how we were baptised, or how comprehensive our confession of faith is. The question is whether you love!

The relational aspect of Christianity is therefore of the utmost importance to the security of your soul. There can be nothing more important than that.

No matter which denomination you belong to, how good the congregational worship is, how many areas of ministry you have worked in, how accurate your belief or how extensive your Bible knowledge, the question remains, do you love?

First of all, do you love Christ? The Bible proof that you love Christ is not merely saying that you love Him, or even feeling that you love Him. It is possible to deceive yourself into thinking that you love Christ, even while you have all sorts of lovely feelings about Him. No, the Bible test is, do you love the brethren?

> *"This is how we know what love is: Jesus Christ laid down his life for us. And we ought to lay down our lives for our brothers."* (1 John 3:16)

CHAPTER-ELEVEN

COMMUNITY, *not* DEMOCRACY

"He who receives you receives me,
and he who receives Me receives the one who sent me."
Matthew 10: 40

Democracy does not produce community. Contrary to the assumptions of many people, and the doctrines of some denominations, democracy and community are not of the same make-up – in fact, they are more often than not of a contrary spirit. Put bluntly, democracy does not, and cannot, produce true community. It might produce pseudo-community, and it has no doubt taken that form in very many places, but will not by its nature produce true community.

We mentioned earlier the incompatibility of law and grace when discussing vows and covenants. We have the same issue of non-compatibility similarly at work here. The decisions of a majority in a democratically governed church, which then become the law by which all are governed, is again a legalistic structure rather than a grace. Democracy might look like grace, but it is not, in principle, grace.

None of this is a comment on political processes, or the best form of government for nations, as I also commented on briefly in an earlier book. I am not at this point discussing democracy with respect to anything other than the life of the church.

We found that to achieve community, we had to get rid of democracy. This was one of the things the Lord led us to do in the lead up to the revelation that there is an *anointing* by which community is built. You will remember from our story that we spent seven years looking to build community, and thought we had failed, until we found that anointing. The truth is, of course, that in those seven years we learned many things, and made many changes, which prepared the way for the Holy Spirit to move upon us with the anointing in 2002. One of the things we discovered was this issue of the struggle between democracy and community.

In 1988, when I was invited to become the senior pastor of what was a Baptist church, this was a church that constitutionally had always had congregational government. In addition, the church had, through previous struggles and infighting, developed a culture in which leadership was not always to be trusted. This tended to show, not so much in prayer meetings and worship services, but always in the regular Members' Meetings, where all decisions (even the smallest) were made or ratified. When I became the pastor, the Lord gave a grace for me to provide an inspirational leadership for the church which people tended to trust from the heart. By this apostolic grace, there were very few decisions we took in 12 years of those members' meetings that were not in the end unanimous, and nearly so on the other occasions.

It was in 1998, after 10 years of apostolic revelation shared with the church, that the members themselves were asking me to do something about changing the Constitution. I remember Pam Jones, a mature lady who with her husband Elwyn had been Baptist since 1973, coming to see me in my office – and what she had to say was very clear. We had to write a new Constitution for the church, and remove congregational government, because we needed to establish apostolic government. Her views were not untypical. The following year, in the light of what we had learned, I did write a new constitution.

One of the things that clarified our purpose was a prophetic word that came, again through the members, which said we were giving birth to twins. The twins, as it turned out, were 'apostolic life' and an 'apostolic structure' for the church. The message of the Lord at that time was that there needed to be not only new wine, but a new wineskin; and both were necessary, for it was essential that we develop a structure suitable for our doctrine. And we have enjoyed the blessing of that new constitution ever since.

The new constitution removed congregational government and democracy as a principle of church life, but sought to very much appreciate and allow for the development of community alongside of anointed apostolic leadership. The very telling thing is that, under the new constitution, there has been such peace and harmony in the life of the church, and moreover, with the awarding of Biblical authority to leadership, that authority has never needed to be used in a unilateral sense. By that, I mean, I have not had to use the authority the Constitution gave me, whereas previously, under a congregational-government type constitution, I had to work hard to have my viewpoint and gift of leadership bear fruit in taking the church in the direction the Lord wanted. The new constitution clarified the authority issue, and like in a good home and good family with good parents, there is no question over the appropriate parental authority in the house. Peace and harmony prevail in a good home where the husband and father, with love, understands how to lead. This fathering authority, in partnership with his wife, puts boundaries in place for the children. They will, on the whole, have a very peaceful home.

The denomination of which we were a part did not like our new constitution. A delegation came to visit us, and I was very surprised to discover their viewpoint. I must have been naive, but it would never have occurred to me to realise how rigid their position was. They said we had to give them major concessions on our Constitution or they were going to put us out of the Baptist Union (and this to a church which, by Baptist polity, was competent to judge it own affairs and govern itself). I had been with them for 12 years, and they had never taken such a nonnegotiable position over any other issue. They had questioned me at times over the years on my points of view concerning the baptism of the Holy Spirit, tongues, healing, worship, and other things, but at no point could they ever conclude that my position was not thoroughly Biblical, and therefore to be allowed as "Baptist". But on the issue of congregational government, they would give no ground at all.

Thus we came to the parting of our ways. In the end, we had an apostolic vision, not only of church government, but of mission, and in separating from the denomination, which we had never planned, we found a greater freedom. Within months we began to experience breakthrough after breakthrough.

In the midst of this process I was seeking the Lord, because these denominational officials had tried to make a strong point about democracy being Biblical and, for them, an important part of New Testament church life. Their appeal was to two incidents in Scripture, both found in the Acts of the Apostles – in Chapter 6, the selection of deacons for the feeding of widows in Jerusalem, and in chapter 15, the Jerusalem Council. Both of these passages, by the way, are narrative rather than teaching, from which we are not meant, according to their more conservative hermeneutics, to define doctrine anyway. Their position was that these were classic examples of democracy at work in the government of the church.

It was over this question that I was seeking the Lord, because everywhere else I looked in the New Testament I saw, not democracy, but apostolic leadership at work – an apostolic leadership which greatly enjoyed the cooperation of the believers. And yet here were these two stories. I laid it before the Lord, and my question of God was, "How is it that we have these two examples of democracy in the New Testament when everything else looks apostolic?" The Lord spoke immediately: ***"Not democracy, community!"***

I got the point. These are not examples of democracy at all, but rather examples of community at work under apostolic leadership. In the case of the choosing of the deacons, it was a directive of the apostles being carried out. They gathered the saints, told them to choose the best qualified from amongst themselves, and gave responsibility to them for organising the practical task of the equitable distribution of food to the neglected Grecian widows. That is not democracy; that is delegation within community life. In Acts Chapter 15, when the greatest and most potentially divisive issue of all came up in the life of the church, they gathered the entire senior ministry leadership – the apostles and elders. It is true there was a very lengthy discussion, probably heated. Again this was not democracy, and no vote was taken. As in real community life, everyone can be listened to, all insights are weighed up, but in the end the anointed leadership must lead. In the Jerusalem Council, after much discussion, Peter addressed them and presented the incisive word that brought the discussion to a focus, and Barnabas and Paul then enjoyed the silent attention of the gathering, after which James the chairman of the meeting and leader of the Jerusalem church, made a decision. His very words were, *"It is my judgement, therefore, that we..."* (Acts 15: 19) Don't accept the nonsense that this was democracy at work.

We should go back to the word the Lord gave me, and see it as a guiding principle. He said, "Not democracy, community." These two things can look very similar on the outside, but democracy will never produce true community. Democracy may appear to have the values of community, but its underlying principles will destroy the trust and intimacy that are essential for the building of true community. In true community the people trust their leaders (not without openness, transparency, honesty and accountability – in other words, not without reason, and not without personal knowledge of them), but they do trust them. And in community, the people trust each other (*"love,"* as Paul said, *"always trusts."*). This provides the life in which all can share, all can speak, all can contribute, and all are loved, but in the end, like a good Mum and Dad in the home, there is an obligation upon leadership to seek the Lord and with the good of their people at heart, lead. This produces the happy home which we know as Christian community.

You can try democracy all you like, but it will never take you past pseudo-community. At the same time, you will still have all the trouble and chaos along the way that democracy can never shield you from – but community will take you beyond it.

The Lord's Table

I do not wish to close without including a brief word about something very practical and tangible. The powerful community effect of the Lord's table upon a fellowship.

Like baptism, which we mentioned earlier as having a significant role to play, so too is the celebration of Holy Communion, shared by the church in fellowship, a powerful means of grace. Whilst baptism is, usually, a once-for-all entering into a grace, sharing in the table of the Lord must be regularly maintained.

The church has always known these things to be a 'means of grace,' even though we have not always understood or agreed about what it means or how it works. But if baptism is that act of submission in which something is really shifted off our lives after receiving the saving grace of Christ, then Holy Communion is a powerful glue that helps to hold the life of the fellowship together. I mean by this, there is an actual power and presence of the Lord in it for this very purpose. I cannot treat this subject at length here, and hope to return to it for a fuller treatment later. But the apostle Paul said quite explicitly (1 Corinthians 10: 16-17) that the cup for which we give thanks is a *"participation"* in the blood of Christ, and the bread which we break is a *"participation in the body of Christ."* He adds, incisively, that by this, *"we, who are many, are one body, for we all partake of one loaf."*

The word 'participation' here (in other translations, 'communion', or 'sharing') for me indicates an active, dynamic, joining together. It has been a matter of discovery through personal experience that this act of sharing around the table of the Lord somehow does effectively hold people together in divine fellowship. Without defining it too closely, there is actual power present in the table of the Lord, usually unseen and unfelt, but it is power nevertheless. It is more than just a memorial, as some would have it; it is an actual means of grace, and I am of the belief, based on these years of experience, that without a very regular use of the table of the Lord, the life of the church *as a people* becomes 'thin on the ground,' – it becomes somehow scattered, and there progressively grows a sense of threat against the security of the people staying together.

We moved years ago from a once-a-month celebration of the Lord's Supper to an every-Sunday celebration, specifically because we found this to be an important and dynamic part of church life, which directly affected that sense of the church membership being glued together. The Scriptures do say, *"From him the whole body, joined and held together by every supporting ligament, grows and build itself up in love, as each part does it work."* (Ephesians 4: 16) The Table of the Lord is one of those things through which, *"from him,"* something consistently comes by which we are *"held together."*

I personally think you cannot maintain the closeness of which I speak in any Christian community without the Table of the Lord being properly used – and I have come to this point of view late in life, so to speak, since I was raised in a non-sacramental denomination. It took years to gct past my assumptions that it was simply a meaningful ceremony designed to focus the church constantly on the central fact of our faith. It does this too, but what I was to discover is its intrinsic and dynamic power, which produces what is obviously an intended effect, that by the presence of the Lord in the Table, there is given a grace that somehow anoints and blesses the people to be and remain *"one body,"* not in a theoretical theological sense, but in the very outworking of them being connected, and being in love as *"members of one another."* (Ephesians 4: 25)

CHAPTER-TWELVE

Practical Steps To Building *Community*

A Guide for Leaders

"Command and teach these things.
Don't let anyone look down on you because you are young,
but set an example for the believers in speech,
in life, in love, in faith, and in purity."
1 Timothy 4:12

I would like to offer some practical steps by which pastors and church leaders can feel positive about working and praying towards establishing 'community.' Having pondered this before the Lord, I set out here steps I feel are important, even essential, to creating the circumstances under which churches might be led in the appropriate direction, and grace might be obtained from the Lord and established permanently in church life.

1. Change Values

Teaching is essential to establish the values needed for change. We observed earlier that there was no Pentecost until after Jesus taught the disciples His values, and even though His followers were without power to live that way, the truth was established in their hearts.

We need to put into the hearts of our people fresh convictions about the way believers conduct themselves in the household of faith. Our problem is that our people are often full of values that have been handed down from institutionalised Christianity. The old pastoral-care mindset that the pastor has to do everything for the members, for example, is one thing that does have to be greatly modified. There are mindsets about how the church is to operate that have to be changed. One of them, democracy, will need to be adjusted.

The 'new' values we are to teach are *relational* values, and will include concepts of sonship and fathering, of generational blessing, of community, of what it means to walk with one another, and of apostolic covering and apostolic grace.

2. Don't Change Structures before you Change Values

This step is super-critical. Do not change structures in your church or ministry until you have successfully changed the values. This wisdom didn't begin with me - many others say this too.

If you suddenly change the structure of your church, without first addressing what people believe about how the church should operate, how it should be structured, what we do or don't do, etc, you are asking for trouble. So it is wise, and generally essential, to teach the values needed for change, then you can change the structures without too much pain and loss.

Back in the 90s, I taught our church apostolic values by constantly sharing the apostolic revelation as I received and grew in it - and made no attempt at all to change the constitution of the church, or even suggest it. After some years we got to the point where I had Baptists, one after another, saying we had to change the constitution. We then presented a new constitution, which removed democracy completely, for the approval of the members. We took a vote, to stop voting, and the vote was unanimous. Everyone hungered for it because we had successfully changed their values. So pastors and teachers have a very important part to play.

People not only *act* in accordance with what they believe, which helps you bring in change, people will also pray, and therefore receive answers to prayer, on the basis of what they believe. So if we are properly teaching apostolic values, we are more likely to see apostles emerge by the grace of God. If you are teaching the values of sonship, and teaching the Pentecostal grace of community, you are more likely to see these things come to pass in the lives of your people.

3. The Leader must be a 'Son'

I am speaking specifically to senior leaders on this point, but this truth is for us all. I don't think you will have success in the building of community, unless sonship is established as a primary foundational value – which means, it has to be in the heart of the senior leader. You yourself must be a 'son' in the ministry.

It will do no good, and is not right in principle anyway, for a pastor to be promoting the idea of others being a son to him, but he or she is not a son to anybody. It is the church leadership especially which needs to walk in the spirit of sonship.

That means you must recognise a God-given relational leadership in place over yourself in the ministry. You must have, or establish, a fathering relationship in your own life, and receive fathering love. All senior leaders need to walk with a spiritual father, and give their hearts fully to such a relationship.

This step is quite critical to genuinely establishing community effectively. You must pursue relationships, and pursue a spiritual father, because you will not reap what you do not sow. If you want to reap good relational things in your own congregation, if you want a relational atmosphere, then the senior leader will need to be committed to personally exploring rich relationships. Therefore, you must pursue a spiritual father.

William Booth, the founder of The Salvation Army, in answer to a question from a pastor who was not having much success with his unresponsive congregation, gave this advice: "If you want them to bleed, you will have to haemorrhage." What he meant was, for example, if you want them to pray with passion, you will have to pray with more passion. For us in this context, I am saying, if you want others around you to be sons in the house, you yourself must be a great son in the ministry.

4. Supplication - Prayer that brings Change

Supplication is a word we don't use much anymore,

but it means strong, heart-felt petition and intercession. Supplication is that kind of prayer which refuses to be denied, crying out to God, even with tears. Jesus prayed with loud cries and tears, and was heard because of his reverent submission. This is supplication – a prayer that is desperate in holding on to God. If you want community to develop, and want the Holy Spirit to move upon your people with power, there is no substitute for seeking God.

Pentecost was preceded by ten days of fervent, united prayer. We noted there could be no Pentecost without three years of teaching values, but really, there could be no Pentecost without the church being in prayer prior to the coming of the Holy Spirit. Therefore, we have a Biblical pattern we can follow.

5. Release the Anointing

Learn to release this anointing. It is not a difficult thing to do. At the end of every meeting where you teach on a suitable theme, step out in faith. Choose to believe that, in Christ's name, you can receive from the throne of grace an anointing, and bring that anointing down upon the congregation. Release it over them, and it will bear fruit.

I would suggest that pastors make it a regular practice to release the anointing that builds community (and you will be able to release other anointings too). It will be like regularly putting fertiliser on your fields in anticipation of a better harvest.

Years ago, there was a Sunday when I felt led to do this with a different grace. Our church had seen great progress in healings, with wonderful and miraculous answers to prayer. But in the same church there was virtually nothing of the prophetic in any form. One Sunday around 1992, I felt led to simply pray over the church and command that the eyes of their hearts would be opened to see in the spirit, and I released that prophetic anointing. I didn't see anything happen on the day, just like the day 10 years later when I released the community anointing. But within two years of having released the anointing for prophetic giftedness, our church was full of it. Now we have a church where everyone contributes in the area of hearing the Lord, getting words and insights, and seeing visions and interpreting dreams. This became a natural part of everyday church life, but it built up from the time I released the anointing for the purpose, on a normal Sunday morning.

I think all five-fold ministers can exercise this kind of leadership authority and release anointings. I think Christians generally can do this in their own sphere of authority. What will make the difference is faith, i.e. what we believe.

6. Keep on Teaching Sonship and Community

Keep on teaching the values of sonship and community. Come back to it consistently, because you have a goal in mind. There are many other things a pastor will have to teach, but these truths will need to be established and held as values by many people, because really you are looking for a pearl of great price.

7. Address Financial Commitment

In June, 2009, I heard the Lord say: "There is never any effective community where there is no financial commitment."

Fortunately, I have regularly taught financial foundations to our people, and it must have helped a great deal. Christians are not really living as Christians if they do not know how to give. Without giving, there can be no spiritual maturity and no victory.

The most basic financial foundation is the tithe, but there are some, here and there, who speak against tithing by assuming it to be Old Testament law. But not so. It is a New Covenant grace, which is best and easily taught from the New Testament, although to prevent it from being treated legalistically it does not appear in the New Testament in the form of a command. Tithing predated the law as a principle of life with Abraham and the patriarchs, whose footsteps of faith we walk in. Of course it was included in the law of the Old Covenant, as was every good thing, such as, *"Love the Lord your God..."* Just because something appears in the law of the Old Covenant, does not mean it is not also a grace, both prior to the law, and in the New Covenant. Hebrews 7 tells us that under the Law, tithes were collected from the Israelites by their brothers the Levites, but in the New Covenant, the tithe is collected *"...by him who is declared to be living,"* i.e. the risen Christ. (Hebrews 7: 5, 8)

The tithe has a very specific purpose for us, but it is not a form of giving, since the tithe is not ours; it belongs to the Lord. We do not give tithes as gifts; we *return* the tithe to the Lord. By this we show our trust and submission to Him, by giving back what is His. The key significance of the tithe, as it always has been, is submission to Lordship. Tithing is a tremendous power dynamic, totally different to offerings.

The act of consistently, regularly, and accurately tithing, positions us in a practical and real way relative to the sovereign power and grace of the Lordship of Christ.

When we tithe, we are doing more than just saying, "Jesus is Lord" (which can be no more than 'lip service' if it is without corresponding action), and puts some decision-making over money right where we say our heart is. Tithing is the ultimate reality in showing our submission, because it is tangible, involves a powerful issue of the heart, and is a constant, i.e. it is a trust we maintain. And to do it does require trust, as well as obedience. This powerfully and demonstrably positions you under the sovereign protection of having Lordship in place as a reality established by obedience, and not just a faith theory, and thereby activates the protections spoken of in Malachi 3: 11, *"I will prevent pests from devouring your crops, and the vines in your fields will not cast their fruit."*

The tithe might not always bring increase, but it sure protects you from a lot of losses. This is why it is true to say that the tithe protects you financially. That is its principal effect, directly related to its place in the faithful believer's life of being the constant, regular, and practical outworking of your declaration that Christ is Lord.

And besides, there are some churches that could really use the promise regarding pests and crops, and vines and fruit. We are God's field, and we need our harvest of righteousness in the lives of our people protected.

What do we do with the tithe? The tithe is meant to follow the route of primary anointings. Someone should always be seen as being over you in the Lord, and they represent Christ to you. The tithe is an act of submission to the Lordship of Christ, and therefore should be submitted to those in authority. The person tithing submits it, meaning they yield authority over how it is used, to another. In churches, every member brings their tithes so that in an act of corporate oneness we return our tithes. What of the senior minister, and the church ministry. They need to submit their tithes to the support of those who exercise the responsibility of the primary anointing over them, i.e. your apostolic covering. Our tithe should always flow in the direction of the authority Christ has placed over us in the ministry.

There is real power and grace in thc tithe, and for us, this seemed to increase when we began to use the tithe as a tithe rather than as an offering, by properly using it for the support of those over us. Every month I make sure my tithe is released to my apostolic covering. From time to time, I remind our people of the important place of the tithe in our lives. Over and above that, we have the responsibility and opportunity of living life as generously as possible.

Above and beyond the tithe we teach generosity and sacrificial giving, because if the heart is not in giving, the heart is not in much at all. Jesus said, *"Where your treasure is, there your heart will be also."* (Matthew 6:21) We usually need to teach believers to give; it is not automatic for most, but learning to give really brings freedom to their hearts, and their heart follows their money in service to Christ.

It would be foolish to say that a local church was a wonderful community if the people would not financially support the community. No, generosity goes hand in hand with this grace. This is very evident in the early church, too, for following Pentecost there was tremendous generosity in the church.

I have made these comments with the local church in mind, but it is also true with respect to our apostolic covering. Every pastor and church needs to relate to an apostle, and there needs to be a financial commitment to that relationship. The Lord wants us to receive the blessing of our apostles, but He requires us to be a blessing to them also. We will receive strength from them, but we must strengthen them in return. (1 Corinthians 9:11) A financial relationship opens the channel of God's blessing all the more.

It is not that you are buying anything, but rather, without a financial commitment you haven't given your heart, and neither have you really respected and given honour. This was the point Jesus made. He did not say that where your heart is, there your money will be also. What Jesus said was, where your treasure is, there your heart will be also.

Unless you address financial issues, you will not be able to build strong community, for remember the principle, there can be no effective community that does not have a financial foundation. If there are members of churches whose hearts are not in their giving, their hearts have not really been given to their brethren, and certainly not to their leaders, and they are not really an effective, participating part of the community.

I would add a further comment for the benefit of leaders – you should sow to the benefit of your own sonship. You are meant to be a son to a father, therefore sow financially into His life and calling.

8. See Yourself as being Under Authority

A deep need is touched here. Again, I am speaking to five-fold ministers in particular, but the principle applies as well to every believer. Every leader needs to see themselves as "a man under authority." This principle applies to every apostle, prophet, pastor, and other ministry; we cannot be a law unto ourselves.

You need to have apostolic covering. It is still early days, and if as yet you have no apostolic covering in place, still you might have some other form of covering. Either way, there is a leadership that you relate to.

In the gospel story of the centurion, he said to Jesus, "*... just say the word, and my servant will be healed.*" (Matthew 8:8) That centurion knew that Jesus had authority to heal because He was, like himself, under authority. Because the centurion was part of an authority structure, he then could exercise authority.

This was a spiritual lesson provided in the gospel for us, for likewise, when you or I live as 'men under authority,' we will then have authority. Thus our lives, our words, and the state of our hearts, will have an effect on those around us. But it is in our own heart, rather than in externals, that each of us is, or is not, "a man under authority."

There are many who do not *see* themselves as being under authority, even though they have others over them in the Lord. There is still independence, and all kinds of fleshly thoughts and selfish desires at work. They have not come to the place of heart submission; they are still operating out of something within that is not Christ-like. But if a leader is going to successfully build community, he must come to see himself as under the authority of another person.

Many years ago, the Lord carefully positioned me in this way. I had dreams and visions in which the Holy Spirit was trying to help me understand this important principle. In one of those dreams, the hair on my head was not my own, it was the hair of the man who became my apostolic father. He has his own particular style and colour, and in my dream, that's what I had on my head. By this symbol the Lord was confirming that I was to be under this man's leadership. I am referring to my spiritual father, Apostle Chuck Clayton.

I have to see myself positioned in this way, having a heart that is for him, and willing to listen to him. I am here to help, serve, honour, and be a blessing to him. In Christ I have a duty to love him, to love what he loves, and to care about what he cares about. So I grew to have the heart of a son, and as my love for him grew, my ability to see things grew. The more I was positioned under that grace of authority, the more freedom I had, and the more blessings I received. Because I am a son and a man under authority, there are many things that have come to me, and many ways in which I have seen the increase of the favour of God. Every pastor needs to see the principle of this matter, and come to the place of understanding the restoration of apostolic authority in the church.

Apostolic authority must come alongside you, and be at work for you in the church. This is in itself an important key to building community, for apostles do have a particular grace to build relationally. That is what is included in an apostolic anointing. These things were all in place for us prior to getting our breakthrough into community.

9. Establish a Culture of Honour and Affection

The church was always meant to have a culture of honour. We are to lift each other and our leaders up, and in that show great affection for each other. We are to speak highly of others, being careful not to be minimalist with these things. We are to hold our leaders dear, high in our esteem, for Christ's sake. (1 Thessalonians 5: 12-13)

If you want to reap honour, then you will need to sow it. Not only that, but an example must be set by the leaders.

Paul, in writing to Timothy, said, "*...set an example for the believers...*" (1 Timothy 4:12) Leaders will always need to be a model for others.

Besides all this, it is honourable to give honour. It is not noble to withhold honour; the truly noble person gives honour easily. The person who has grace knows how to show affection to another person. Some of us, however, do not find it easy to do this. We hold ourselves back, and find we don't have freedom of speech. We would like to say nice things, but we are embarrassed or don't feel warm enough emotionally. This problem needs to be overcome.

The way to address issues of character and overcome each problem is to bring them to the cross and pray them through. The power of the cross does a deep work in us, and we become men and women of honour, so that we receive others well, and give them honour in the eyes of the church.

Some people have other reasons for not giving honour. They are jealous of the other person, or they are ambitious. They think they are better than others, and so they do not like to speak highly of them. Those who struggle like this have a spiritual problem; something in the heart has to be cleaned away. We should be able to greatly honour other people, uphold them in the eyes of others, and express our respect for others, so that we become men and women of honour.

The Bible is clear enough. We are to honour each other more than ourselves. (Romans 12:10) We have, then, a Biblical mandate to honour. These are values that need to be taught to the whole church. They will help determine the way we think, believe, and act. There will never be real community without honour, and the senior leader must open the way and set the example. He must sow what he wants to reap, and in so doing will change the culture of the church.

There can be no half measures; we must give an abundance of honour. If you minimise it so that there is just enough honour given to be well-mannered, then you hinder the process. In fact, sometimes it is quite harmful to give only a 'measured' compliment, rather than a heart-felt one. The Scripture says *"love one another deeply from the heart."*(1 Peter 1:22) There is no reason why "deeply, from the heart" cannot mean emotional, earnest, and passionate – I think it should.

We must have a big heart for other people. It will be an important task to establish, maintain, and defend principles of honour and affection in the church.

10. Purposefully Operate out of Apostolic Values

We must consciously and purposefully operate out of apostolic values. The problem with human nature, though, is that often we accept new ideas in our thoughts, but don't yet have them in the heart. We might desire to see things done a new way, but still tend to act out of the old ingrained habitual patterns of thinking.

It may be that a pastor hears the apostolic teaching about apostolic covering and sonship. He comes to understand, too, that we should build the church relationally, and for this to happen, many changes will have to take place. He believes this and knows it is true, and he begins to teach his church accordingly.

One Sunday he teaches that they must think differently and act differently. Then, on Monday or Tuesday, some situation comes up and he has to make a decision. He is not especially thinking now about what he preached, and simply responds in the way he always has – the old way. He doesn't stop and think about how things should be done based on the new beliefs; he just maintains the old system. This is a conundrum; it happens everywhere, and can go on for years. There are pastors who believe they are apostolic and teach apostolic things on Sunday but still run the whole church the old way during the week.

Over the years, we have invited many people to visit our home and stay with us for a few days. When they are with us, we talk, have meals together, pray for them, and show them around. All this is normal for us – other work is laid aside, and we spend our time with them. We didn't realise how significant this was until one particular man came for a visit.

He is a very godly man, highly respected, has a large church and a great reputation, and he spent two days with us. As he was leaving, he told us that we'd had a tremendous impact on him, and the time with us had transformed his life. We found that hard to believe, because we hadn't done anything special apart from basic friendship. But he had said that his life had been profoundly changed, so after he left we asked the Lord some questions.

Why did this man say he was so profoundly changed? Why did he feel it so deeply? The Lord gave us an answer. He said that many people talk about relationships but they don't change the way they live, whereas we try to *live* relationships. When people come to visit, the main subject is not business; we give our time. Many others talk much about relationships but don't change their programme or their agenda. Their lifestyle, and the way they spend their time, remains the same.

If we would build relationally, our main business becomes relationships; it is not to be just a theory, but the way we live. It is for this reason that, when we spend time with someone, they feel it in the heart, and grace is at work. This challenge means not merely talking about relationships, but changing priorities, and considering just how we will go about the business of building leadership in the church. This is foundational to operating out of apostolic values.

11. Temper Expectations

I am told that John Wesley went to visit Count Zinzendorf, and came away disappointed. He went because he had seen the fabulous outworking of the grace that was on the Moravian families he had met in his travels. He was so impressed by their profound faith, courage, and spirituality, as well as their devotion and sacrifice, and also their accomplishments, that he wanted to meet the man, and see for himself.

During Wesley's visit, he was given the task of working in Zinzendorf's vegetable garden. And for Wesley, nothing happened, there was nothing to see, and he went away disappointed and somewhat critical. This is because idealistic expectations will always wrong-foot us from finding the grace that is there, because the outcome of having 'expectations' is that we look for outward things that you can see with the human eye. It does not work that way.

This grace is a hidden thing, and if people come to visit, it will tend to be seen much more clearly by those who are not looking for it as something that glows. It's as if you can see it if you do not have idealistic expectations – but if you have some kind of perfectionist idealism, you will be blind-sided from recognising it, and if you have a judgmental heart, you may be kept from finding it.

Advice for Visitors

If anyone chooses to visit us, my advice to them has been, don't come looking for outward things. Just come looking to be at home with people; the idea is to connect. The whole point should be to spend time in the communion of fellowship, that is, meaningful time with people. And that is when the grace flows. Like the dew, it appears.

I shared with you just now the story of that dear brother, a highly respected Christian leader, who, having spent two days in our home, remarked as he was leaving that we had profoundly changed his life. We hadn't done anything except drink coffee and eat meals together, and in conversation share our lives. But the anointing, the dew of heaven, is found in the relationship; it is in the time we have for each other. How could we make the point that the two great outcomes of community are the removal of striving on the one hand, and the admiration of each other on the other hand, unless it is the actual interaction of people that we are referring to.

12. Deal with Idealism, Perfectionism, Judgements, and Criticism.

Years ago, at around the same period we made these big breakthroughs, we went through a period that was difficult. Our people were struggling somewhat, they seemed flat and unable to rise, and it was a hard time to move ahead. It was a period in which things seemed a bit heavy as far as leading the ministry was concerned. The memory is a bit vague to me now, but at the time it was a burden, and I was left wondering. With all our prayer, and ideals, and encouragement for our people, with all our love, exhortation, and teaching, why did things seem to be dragging?

And then the light dawned, for the Lord gave me a word and opened my eyes to what was causing it. I had amongst my team of leaders a number who tended to be perfectionist and too idealistic, and as a result, critical and judgemental. The problem was, these issues did not appear in a really obvious way, meaning, we did not see these leaders that way. That was because we were close, they were friends, they were totally committed and dedicated and hard-working, they loved the Lord, and were very much a part of everything we were doing. And they were humorous, too. But once I saw it for what it was, it became clear what our problem was. They had been raised with very high ideals about Christian service, and how Christians should perform for the church. They had set high standards upon themselves, and held them for everyone else too. And when anyone didn't measure up, they felt somewhat aggrieved, and as time went on would express critical judgements. Sometimes the condemnation was just a humorous aside, and sometimes it was a straight out criticism, such as, "They never...," or "They always..."

What I saw, to my horror, was that our work to love our people, and to lift them up, had, for at least some time, been hindered and quashed by the 'opinions' or attitudes of some of the strongest supporters I had in the leadership. The work of God was being cursed, and it was coming from judgements about how people were not performing.

I imagine that the health and success of many churches and people groups all over the world are at times cursed by the judgements of their own leaders, who can very easily, out of frustration, and disappointment that things have not gone well, speak definitive words that curse. Often these are words of complaint or observation (and leaders do need to make honest observations and assessments), but their words can also come from a spirit of disappointment, or fleshly standard-setting, and so we get such opinions as, "They always let me down," or "They shouldn't have done this," or "They should have done that," or "They never measure up," or "They are never there when you need them," and so on.

I would warn leaders that your own judgements, but just as easily the judgements of your staff, members of your pastoral team, or other key leaders, can be cursing the very work you are seeking to bless – as can the words or attitudes of others in the fellowship, too.

At the time, I raised this issue thoughtfully with my team. I wanted them to see for themselves how harmful their own personality and spiritual assumptions might have been upon our work. And I needed everyone's cooperation in prayer and repentance to remove the 'curse' and change unintended but destructive habits that were hidden in amongst bright and strong personalities. And when these things come, as they will for us all, though only a few have made the mistake, we all repent together, and do so as if each one of us is personally the offender. We dealt with it properly and tenderly, and continue to guard our hearts as we go along.

If pastors or leaders remark to me, as they have at times, that their people are not doing as well as they should, my reply is usually, "It's not their fault, it's yours." I say this only to get enough 'attention' to then make the point that pastors and leaders must avoid putting blame as a judgement on others, while accepting the responsibility of so praying for their people, and so loving them, that there is, or soon will develop, a greater grace to take their people further on the journey – and we rejoice much in the meantime, for we may as well enjoy the journey. Do not expect your followers to perform to the level of your own spirituality, and then judge them for their failures, or blame them for the slow progress of the church, if they don't measure up. Instead, take the attitude, "It is my task to pray and love them into a better place." Persevere. And especially persevere with finding grace for yourself. There is no joy to be found anywhere in always looking for others to live up to our expectations. We curse ourselves, too, when we do that. I'd rather have the joy of seeing Christ in people. We need eyes for that.

So be careful to thoughtfully clean out any spirit of criticism or judgement you might find amongst your own people, whether against your own people or others. I think there is nothing more harmful than the condemnation of people by those appointed to love them.

Remember, It's a Great Grace in Ordinary Lives

It is interesting how, under the grace of this anointing that brings peace, security, love, and affection, and in particular the absence of striving, to a group as a whole, believers are still free to be themselves, and as in all of life, individuals and families have their ups and downs. The fact that some individual or family has to work an issue through, or has a serious problem in their character that needs to be addressed, all of which takes time, does not undermine the wholeness of the group as a people. Even the struggling ones have a great sense of belonging and of love. So there remains room for people to be natural, with their faults and weaknesses, and the need for them to grow and learn and change, whilst at the same time there is present such a wonderful grace for peace along with that wonderful freedom of belonging without striving.

The grace of the community anointing doesn't instantly perfect the saints, and does not necessarily remove the normal, and healthy, struggles of life – in which we are here for each other. You could have a church with an Ananias and Saphira in the midst, but that does not mean that grace is not upon the whole.

13. Note the Important Place of Weakness

Consider the following Scriptures:

> *"On the contrary, those parts of the body that seem to be weaker are indispensable...*
> *...God has combined the members of the body and has given greater honour to the parts that lacked it, so that there should be no division in the body, but that its parts should have equal concern for each other."* (1 Corinthians 12: 22-25)

> *"But he said to me, 'my grace is sufficient for you, for my power is made perfect in weakness.' Therefore I will boast all the more gladly about my weaknesses, so that Christ's power may rest upon me. That is why, for Christ's sake, I delight in weaknesses... For when I am weak, then I am strong."*
> (2 Corinthians 12: 9-10)

Speaking of weaknesses, many of the people we will work with, who will be totally devoted to you and each other and to the ministry of Christ, will have weaknesses which you might wish they did not have. Some of these will have quite opposite personalities, too. Not only that, but as a whole, most of us are very ordinary people – we do not usually have amongst us a lot of powerful, high-performance-in-ministry kind of people. Rather it is as a people together, as a team, as an apostolic company, that we will achieve something. And that brings me to what I want to explain.

The apostle Paul makes plain that our weaknesses are most important to us, and the weakest member is the one who is the really indispensable part of the body. I think this is true, not just in the sense of being a nice doctrine to have because Jesus loves us all, but because it is a functioning reality with an actual, practical, dynamic, outworking in the body.

I have come to see that the weaknesses we have had amongst us have served us well in many ways. By 'weaknesses' I am not referring to sin or moral failure, but things such as inefficiency, poor communication skills, personality faults, rigidity, and the like. It was because of weaknesses that we have had to go slower on some things, or work patiently with someone needing to progress in their role, or persevere with someone needing to address a personality fault, or handle discussions more thoughtfully, or go over things again. As a result, tenderness, caring, thoughtfulness, mutual respect, patience, and willingness to take time over decisions – these are some of perhaps many things that have grown within us, without us realising it was going on, and have helped, I think, to establish honour as well.

I think it is only as we accept, remain committed to, love and lift up, regard as equals, and honour as better than ourselves, the members with weaknesses, that as a body we progressively change, and in the process become far more like the kind of people we are crying out to be. And we end up not just more Christ-like in the sense that we might appear to be nice, and act nicely, but in the sense that we do then carry, usually without realising it ourselves, a far greater sense of "God in the midst." So rather than becoming exasperated over somebody's weakness, which we all tend to do, we can instead rejoice in the ways of God, while at the same time endeavouring to help people see their need and overcome their weakness.

The exception to all of this has to do with what the Bible calls a heretic (KJV), a factious (NASB) or divisive person (NIV).

14. Exclude Divisive Persons

> *"Warn a divisive person once, and then warn him a second time. After that, have nothing more to do with him. You may be sure that such a man is warped and sinful; he is self-condemned."* (Titus 3: 10-11)

There are those who harm the body and, if left on the loose, will cause deception and spiritual hurt to others. They carry with them and will bring into the fellowship a spirit of lawlessness, sometimes in the form of a Jezebel or Absalom spirit, and many of these carry a strong spirit of witchcraft and seduction. Be discerning and thoughtful, because at first appearance people like this can look good – and they will be excited about the church, and complimentary, and supportive, and gifted. They are often manipulative and controlling, but slyly so, until they gain influence through friendships. Sometimes you see it for what it is on the first day, but it can take 18 months, and sometimes more, to find what is in some people. Our members themselves are very quick these days to discern these problems in anyone coming in, and we confront them graciously, but quickly, to instruct, inform, and draw the boundaries. I often have our 'weakest' brothers do this for me.

There have to be boundaries. Every household requires discipline, and the last thing I want is someone new coming in the door carrying a seductive spirit of witchcraft or control, all slyly hidden in a package claiming to be prophetic, which if accepted by us would work to destroy what we have - and the longer they hang around without being confronted or exposed, the more they build the power of a seductive spirit. We have to be alert, and quick to confront. We explain sonship, and we explain submission. If we win a brother or sister, and they submit, and repent, and are willing to learn, and seek to change – well and good. If not, and they leave immediately, or within a few weeks, we have done a good job; we have guarded the door of the sheep-fold as the shepherds appointed by Christ, and have acted to protect the flock. (Acts 20: 28, 1 Peter 5: 1-4)

Discipline in churches is absolutely crucial, and the longer we leave some things, the worse they get, especially if we allow the free-ranging of anyone with a division spirit. Paul said to warn them, and warn them again, and after that have nothing more to do with them. (Titus 3:10-11) When these kinds of people will not receive correction or submit to the authority and integrity of the house, there is no choice; they have to leave.

Teachableness is crucial. If any brother or sister is not a teachable person, you can do nothing with them. They will waste your time, they will harm the lives of others, and they will bring in influences and ideas that you do not want. You must never build with them, and never, ever, give them authority or position, There are people like this who will talk big, claim to have a lot of spiritual knowledge, or claim to be speaking the truth, and speaking for Christ – and it is all nonsense. Any unteachable person who seeks to actively participate in ministry or speak to the church, you can be sure, is never representing Jesus Christ, no matter what they say. This remains true, even when they are speaking Bible truth. Satan knows the Word of God too, and so do our false brethren. False brethren are not always intending to be deceivers, they are often just deceived.

The principle, then, is to accept the weak, but guard the door against the wolf who is the divisive brother or sister. In these two matters, we seek to do precisely and diligently what the Bible says.

15. Accept the Responsibility for bringing in Change

The changes you desire will not come of their own accord. Leaders do not have the luxury of someone else just doing it all for them. As the leader, the pastor must take responsibility for bringing about the change that is needed. If the church is going to make the transition, resolute leadership will be needed. Therefore, make choices and decisions, win hearts, teach, and cry out to God because you need to see clearly what He wants. Just remember, don't change structures until you have changed values!

Whether we like it or not, God intends to change His people, but He intends to change them through leaders. (I am not speaking of individuals here, but of His people as 'a people.') Some leaders are happy for God to change things, but not necessarily so happy to be the one God uses to bring in the change. But this is God's apostolic method; He doesn't do things Himself when He can work through someone else. God is always the giver of grace. Do the people of God need a deliverer? He will send a deliverer.

God will always try to do His work through someone else, and that person is the sent one of God. That is what an apostle is, and that also is what a pastor is. The children of Israel were suffering much, and they cried out for deliverance. God in heaven heard their cry and came down and appeared to Moses in the burning bush. The Lord said to Moses, "*I have indeed seen the misery of my people... So I have come down to rescue them from the hand of the Egyptians... So now, go. I am sending you to Pharaoh to bring my people out... of Egypt.*" (Exodus 3:7,8,10)

God was not going to carry the rod of God; Moses was going to carry the rod. God would speak to Pharaoh, but only through Moses and Aaron. This is the apostolic method. It may seem humorous that God would say "I have come down to deliver them, therefore you go and deliver them," but that is the way it is.

We find the same thing occurring in the New Testament with Jesus. A big crowd of hungry people had been three days without food, and when the disciples came to Jesus to inform Him that the people were hungry, Jesus first response was, "*They do not need to go away. You give them something to eat.*" (Matthew 14:16) It was only when they did not know how to meet this need, that Jesus said, "*Bring them (the loaves and fishes) to me.*" Similarly, the first response of God to human need is to work or speak through somebody. That is apostolic grace; God always desires that someone represent Him; even in the matter of our salvation.

It was the Father who sent the Son. And when Jesus came, He had two main responsibilities. One was to become our Great High Priest and offer the sacrifice of Himself for our sins. The other was to appoint apostles. He had to train them so that He could give them His authority. Jesus was not going to preach the gospel; He was not even going to stay here. Matthew records (28:19) that He said to the eleven, after His resurrection, *"All authority in heaven and on earth has been given to me. Therefore go..."* That sounds similar, doesn't it, to His words at the burning bush.

Jesus has the responsibility to build the church. Whom will He use? The leaders of the church have been delegated that responsibility, and they need to accept that responsibility; and for this task, Jesus' Spirit, Jesus' anointings, and Jesus' authority have been given to us.

We all need to accept the fact that we have authority on earth to do the will of God, in accordance with our calling; for five-fold ministry, this is, principally, building up the church. In Jesus saying to us, *"All authority... has been given to me. Therefore go,"* the implication is that if you go, all the authority resting on Jesus will rest on you. But you will not find that authority unless you go. There are some things in which we have to step out and obey.

So my word is, take the responsibility to be the deliverer of your people. God sent Moses to Egypt to deliver them, and He is sending you to your people to deliver them. You have authority to preach Pentecost, and to teach the values of Christ-likeness.

Jesus did say to the seventy He sent out ahead to heal and preach in every place He Himself was about to go, "*Go! I am sending you out like lambs among wolves.*" (Luke 10:1-3) That doesn't sound very good, does it? Sometimes, as a leader, it feels like that. You may feel weak and vulnerable, and the people may look ferocious, but trust the grace of God.

One of the best and most effective prayers to pray is a simple one. If ever I have to deal with a difficult situation, I ask God for grace for myself, and for the others, and for the situation itself. Invariably, there is a good outcome. I find that God loves to answer that prayer. The very use of the word 'grace' seems to make God very tender – He can't resist. Ask God for grace for your young people and for families. Ask for grace for your church leaders.

You must try to build everything with grace. The good thing about a prayer like that is that it helps you to stop striving; you are not to trust in yourself.

CHAPTER-THIRTEEN

Apostolic Power, Freedom and Cleansing Judgments

"Therefore judge nothing before the appointed time;
wait till the Lord comes.
He will bring to light what is hidden in darkness
and will expose the motives of men's hearts.
At that time each will receive his praise from God."

1 Corinthians 4:5

"For it is time for judgment to begin with the family of God;
and if it begins with us,
what will the outcome be for those who do not obey the gospel of God?"

1 Peter 4:17

In this final chapter, I am to speak prophetically. Progress has been made toward the restoration of the church as an apostolic people, and there is no turning back the clock. The Church is being renewed, and ordinary believers everywhere are buying into the 'new' values, which are the original values of course, of apostolic rather than institutionalised Christianity. I believe we will see the complete reformation of the church, and the body of Christ will come to the maturity the New Testament calls for before the coming of Christ.

There is to be a great harvest brought into the kingdom of God, but in the form that we have known it, the Church will not receive that harvest. The Church must change, and we are in the business of changing it; this is what apostles and prophets are called to do.

To Rebuild the Ancient Ruins

There is a clear scriptural call, or vision, or mandate, to 'rebuild the ancient ruins'. You will find it spoken of in Isaiah 58:12 and 61:4. This no longer applies in a natural way to the towns and cities of Judea as it did long ago, but now refers, of course, to the church, the body of Christ which *is* the city of God, and which in many ways does in fact lie in ruins across the land. In just about any town or village in the entire world, the broken-down ruins of the Church are to be seen. Instead of a building being properly *"framed together,"* (Ephesians 2:21 KJV) it is in a state of great division, relationally broken into bits and pieces, some of which are called denominations.

In the cities and nations of the world, we see a scattered version of the body – with many believers who are near neighbours having no co-operation or communication with one another at all, and even worse, neither do their leaders. Should there be any wonder there is so little power in the Church! There needs to be a healing of division, but only an apostolic church, i.e. one which has an apostolic life, will be able to find this healing, and begin to bring to the body of Christ the spiritual maturity of that apostolic life, out of which we can multiply, and bear greater fruit in the nations.

In the Acts of the Apostles, we read that new believers were coming in to the church every day; the Church multiplied greatly at that time. However, 'division' is the opposite of multiplication, and we all can see the division in the Church. While ever there is division, we simply cannot achieve the results that we read about in the Acts of the Apostles. Major change must come in answer to our prayers, and for the sake of His Name.

I feel that Psalm 46 is relevant to the subject:

God is our refuge and strength,
an ever present help in trouble.
Therefore we will not fear, though the earth give way
and the mountains fall into the heart of the sea,
Though its waters roar and foam
and the mountains quake with their surging.

There is a river whose streams make glad the city of God,
the holy place where the most high dwells.
God is within her, she will not fall;
God will help her at break of day.

Nations are in uproar, kingdoms fall;
he lifts his voice, the earth melts.
The Lord Almighty is with us;

the God of Jacob is our fortress.
Come and see the works of the Lord,
the desolation he has brought on the earth.
He makes wars cease to the ends of the earth;
he breaks the bow and shatters the spear,
he burns the shields with fire.

'Be still, and know that I am God;
I will be exalted among the nations,
I will be exalted in the earth.'
The Lord Almighty is with us;
the God of Jacob is our fortress."

This psalm speaks prophetically with respect to the last days. When we read, "*there is a river whose streams make glad the city of God,"* most people might think of the New Jerusalem in its final, eternal expression. But on closer examination, the text goes on to say, *"God is within her, she will not fall."* Why would such a thing be said unless there was a threat, or at least a question of the possibility, of her falling? The psalmist is here speaking of something on the earth, made obvious also by the statement, "*God will help her at the break of day.*" Therefore, we should understand that the holy place where God dwells, the church, is going to face a break of day that looks very threatening.

We are Moving Towards that Time

This speaks of something that is to happen on earth, in 'time' rather than eternity. We read of nations being in uproar and the earth melting – we are moving towards that time. The Bible says that it is from the hand of the Lord that both good things and calamity come. (Isaiah 45: 7)

It was Jesus who described the flow of rivers of living water that would come from our innermost being. This is what is being referred to as the streams that make glad the city of God; it is the river of the Holy Spirit that flows from within every one of us.

We are the city of God on the earth, the holy place where the Most High dwells. *"God is within her, she will not fall; God will help her at break of day."* This refers to every time and season in which we His people live, but is especially prophetically pertinent to days ahead. Jesus said there would be great distress on the earth; it is just as well that we have this river whose streams are to make us glad.

We continue to see nations in uproar, and there is more to come. Standing in Africa in the year 2001, I was looking at the strangest sunset I had ever seen. It appeared to be either a terrible, wrathful furnace, or an awesome display of the majesty and glory of God, but what was it? Was it a portent of terrible evil, or a promise of revival? I asked the Lord what it meant, because the Scriptures say He sets signs in the heavens, and we are meant to understand them. His answer was, "From this time, strange and unusual things are going to happen in the world." A few months later, we had that horrifying event take place in New York, on 9/11, the devastation of the twin towers of the World Trade Centre, with a great loss of lives.

But in addition to whatever is happening in the nations, I believe, from what the Lord tells me as well as from the Scriptures, cleansing judgements will be coming upon the Church.

We should not think that we will just go along, day after day, making small gains. I believe that as we complete the task of re-educating the Church and building up a true value system in the hearts of our people, there will come a time when 'critical mass' has been reached, and God will begin to act. That is when we will see judgements come progressively upon the Church – but remember, these are cleansing judgements.

These are Cleansing Judgments

That means they are designed to clean and position the Church. Some time ago, I felt the Lord speak deliberately through Psalm 7, and He applied it to the church.

> *"God is a righteous judge,*
> *a God who expresses his wrath every day.*
> *If he does not relent, he will sharpen his sword;*
> *he will bend and string his bow.*
> *He has prepared his deadly weapons;*
> *he makes ready his flaming arrows."*

We are closer now to the day in which I believe the Lord is going to take up those weapons to deal with the institutionalised Christianity of the world. But we should note that this is not only to deal with what may be in many institutions, but what is in the heart of many leaders and believers in general.

Once, while teaching on this subject (the apostolic reformation of the church) to a gathering of pastors in the city of Sapang Palay, in the Philippines, I experienced a sudden, powerful, physical manifestation of the Holy Spirit as a witness confirming what I was preaching at the time. I would add here that I am a person who virtually never, except for this story, experiences physical 'manifestations' in the body, and for me this was amazing to say the least.

It was as if I was filled with the entire universe, along with shooting stars arcing at great speed through me. It was an explosion of light within, and at the same moment I was filled with the strongest assurance that what I was telling them was absolutely true. What did I say? I had just been proclaiming a word the Lord had given me: that with the release of apostolic grace to the church there would be given also great power, authority, and freedom, but be warned, for concerning the use of that freedom and authority, Christ will judge! And I felt doubly confirmed in that other word He had given me, as explained in my first book, *The Apostolic Revelation*, that an ill wind will blow and shatter the traditional structures of the Church.

Let me restate more specifically what I heard the Lord say: **Along with the release of apostolic grace to the church, great power is about to be given to the people of God; with that power will also be given great authority and freedom. But in the use of that power and freedom, we will bear responsibility, for Christ will judge!**

We are All Asked to Follow Somebody

With respect to true and false apostles and their accountability, I would like to comment that we are each called to follow who we are called to follow, and do what we are called to do. It is not appropriate or proper to have a public discussion or to make a critical assessment of public ministries. They either are, or are not, what they claim to be, and Jesus said that we will know them by their fruit. No one is asked to follow a false leader, but still, all are asked to follow a leader.

If we look at the New Testament, the incidence of failure amongst those genuinely chosen and anointed was very small. Of course, in the Old Testament, there were hordes of false prophets that some kings would have as lackeys, and call in to bring false dreams and visions. However, we are not discussing them; we are here considering those who were called by God and anointed for a task. Very few of those fell from ministry and led people into sin, although there are a few examples, such as Balaam in the Old Testament and Judas in the New Testament, along with one or two lesser characters.

What we do see is a tremendous record regarding the men and women of God who are called and anointed. Naturally, every one of them had faults and failures. If we think about Abraham, David, Peter, and Paul, we see that they had human weaknesses and made mistakes, just as we all do, but every one of them accomplished their purpose because of the grace that was upon them.

One Thing asked of Us is that We Trust

We need to recognise the grace that God is pouring out to raise mighty leaders today. We must avoid being cynical and remember that the one thing asked of us is that we trust. Of course we are not to follow a false leader, but this does not mean that we are not to follow a leader of God's choosing.

The truth is that if we don't trust a leader, then we can never be a part of the building of the house of God. There certainly are a few who are not trustworthy, so we should not trust them. However, this does not relieve anybody of the obligation to find someone that they are meant to trust. The Bible teaches that love always trusts, as we have often heard. We therefore must find leaders, and give our hearts to help them, and be one with them, for Christ's sake. (Hebrews 13: 7, 17)

Some of you have been wounded: you need to forgive, and find healing. Unless you are willing to walk in a trusting relationship with leaders, and with brothers and sisters, you will not be fruitful in the kingdom of God. Instead, that bitterness will create a poison that you will inject into other people.

I have great confidence that God is raising holy prophets and apostles for every land. Having been to many nations, time after time I have found that the Lord has everywhere faithful people who have deep integrity. I thank God that He is raising real and genuine apostolic ministries.

It's All in the Numbers

We have all heard the saying that something is as simple as ABC. For me, this issue is as simple as 1,2,3,4,5,6,7,8,9,10,11,12. What does this mean? It's all in the numbers - 1 Thessalonians chapter 2 and verses 3 to 12. In this passage, Paul is speaking of apostles when he says, *"The appeal we make does not spring from error or impure motives, nor are we trying to trick you. On the contrary, we speak as men approved by God to be entrusted with the gospel. "* (vv 3-4)

Read that whole passage. This is Paul's witness as to what real apostles, including those being raised by God today, are like. And it is by this truth, or this measure, that we can do what the Ephesians did in weeding out the false, as commended by Christ in Revelation 2: 2. Are you going to believe the Word of God, or are you going to believe your bitter memory of some hurt, or be hindered by someone's twisted story? God is raising real apostles today, as He has always done. Even in the first century, a time when no-one disputes there were real apostles, the church had a few con-men trying to take a place among them. This is not an excuse for anyone to cling to unbelief; we all must look to our leaders and serve them.

The fact that somebody has an appearance of apostolic ability, or what looks like an apostolic gift, does not make them an apostle. Some of the cults in the world are led by those who claim to be 'apostles'; we all beg to differ. They are people who have natural gifts that tend to also show up in apostles, but that does not mean that they were ever anointed to be real apostles of Christ. The apostles of Christ that I have known do not turn out like that; they turn out like Peter and Paul. If God trusts these men with the gospel, should we not also trust them?

Paul further said in this passage, *"We are not trying to please men but God, who tests our hearts."* (v. 4b) Most are not aware of it, but genuine apostles continue to be tested throughout the course of their ministries.

Apostles and Authority

God always wants to work through another person. This is why the Father sent the Son. This is central to an apostolic understanding of Christianity. Churches will not be delivered without apostles having been appointed and sent. How are you going to get on if you don't receive the apostle sent to you?

We are not talking about lip-service to apostles here. In this day and age, churches in many places are receiving apostles, but all they are letting them do is be a 'blessing,' and then send them on their way with an offering. Nobody minds if an apostle turns up and preaches a good message, prophesies a good word, and prays a good blessing over the house. Everybody loves them, and the believers are all encouraged and lifted up. But it has to go beyond this in the coming days.

Churches will need to allow for the authority of apostles to be put in place. Again, we are talking a relational authority, not an institutional one – this is an authority in love, a fatherly grace.

And that, I believe, is where the battle in the spirit realm for the advance of the Kingdom of God has got to. It is not any longer a battle over whether the church can have apostles - I think we have won that battle. It is over whether the church will allow apostles to have the authority in leadership they are meant to have. There are people reading this book who need now to have a revelation from the Lord as to how to allow that apostolic authority to do its work. This is meant to be a blessing to you, but real apostles are not going to force it to happen. You have to open the door and receive the grace that is sent to you.

Building Relationally using Apostolic and Prophetic Anointings

Ephesians 2:20 tells us that the apostles and prophets are the foundation of the Church, with Christ Jesus Himself as the chief cornerstone.

When there are no apostles and prophets, or the authority

of these ministries is not recognised and accepted, the only way that we are able to build is to use an institutional method. But when apostolic and prophetic anointings are available, we can build the house of God relationally. The denominationalism that was the natural outcome over hundreds of years of building institutionally, necessary because only pastoral and teaching anointings were recognised and allowed, was a continual replication of institutional division. Five hundred years of this, and there are no less than 35,000 denominations in the world. Building in this kind of way has not produced any great degree of unity in the body of Christ.

When we look at the New Testament, on the other hand, we find that the apostles were very successful in seeing the churches of large cities, with large numbers of Christians in them, built together, from the heart, as one body. This was done in spite of the fact that there were many leaders and teachers, and the people met in many groups. All of the believers in a city knew who their leaders were, and their loyalty and love was towards the elders over the city. The apostles could write to the church of the city, knowing very well that they were addressing the whole church. In those days there was a dynamic at work that enabled the building of a relational church that did not break up into institutionalism. When division did raise its ugly head, the apostles immediately opposed it.

We live in a day when these apostolic and prophetic anointings are being restored in such a way that the Church can be rebuilt; but the building *must* be done relationally. That is, it is very important that we all now learn about these kinds of relationships and are willing to begin to build and walk in them.

Freedom the First Principle of Apostolic Ministry

In forming community or building relationships, it should never be on the basis of anything legalistic, including the making of promises to one another. We must enter these relationships with complete freedom, and that by definition must include the freedom to leave, or it is not freedom.

One of the things I have said to our church repeatedly over past years, and often said long before we knew anything about sonship, fathering, or community, was that "You are free to come in, and you are free to go out. But if you stay, you are here to learn how to walk in relationships with other people. You are to learn how people conduct themselves in the household of faith."

I have always believed that the first principle of apostolic ministry is freedom – that is, the giving of freedom to people; and the goal of the apostle is to bring the people of God into freedom. That is the context in which we build community. People are not to be *obligated*, but must be free. In this way, nothing but the bonds of love hold people together. It is through the changing of the heart that we build the house of God. And for this we need apostles, as well as the apostolic graces of sonship and community, and all their attendant values.

Dear Friends, it just can't be done without Apostles

I have written about community as an obtainable grace, and likewise earlier about sonship. These are graces that are able to transform not only churches, but nations. And there are many who find the teaching of these kinds of subjects acceptable, because they are so sociable. There are things here that every church and tradition will like.

But we have a problem. They come as part of a bigger package, and whilst the concepts may look good when they stand alone, they will lack power if not taken in relationship with the restoration of apostles, apostolic authority, apostolic grace, and the restoration of the apostolic nature of Christianity. In other words, it is part of an overhaul – known as a reformation.

One of the things that Jesus included in His instruction, when explaining that He and His Father were doing a completely New thing to replace the Old, was that we are not to tear a piece of cloth off the new garment to repair the old. (Luke 5:36) Human nature will tend to cherry-pick the bits they like and leave the rest, wanting to improve and repair what they have and can keep control of, rather than moving on. This is that reaction Jesus referred to when He said, concerning the New Wine, that after tasting some will say, "The old is better." But if you want grace and power, you will need to take the new, and take the whole.

Simply put, it is not possible to build a relational Christianity without apostles – they have the grace and the authority for the purpose.

They have the grace? Yes, apostles in particular carry the anointings of Christ for the specific purpose of building His house relationally.

They have the authority? Every house must have some form of authority to hold together. The only question is, will we have a man-made, do-it-yourself kind of authority, which is what we get when we use any of the ways that man feels pleased with. Or do we go with the leadership authority which Christ appoints, and for which we have the Biblical mandate. But if we do not accept the authority structure of

God's appointing, and choose instead some other method, we have, by default, made ourselves the authority.

Christ exercised His father's authority, He spoke in His father's name, and He did the things the Father said to do. Everything He did, He did by the Father's authority, because He had given up His own authority. That is a great humility, the giving up of very large things indeed. After the resurrection, Jesus spoke to His apostles and said, *"All authority in heaven and on earth has been given to me."* (Matthew 28:18) Notice that word, 'given'. During the days of His life on earth, He had great power because of His submission as a Son. After His resurrection, He was given all authority. This grace of submission is the key to apostolic authority in the church.

An apostle is someone who does not represent himself, just as Jesus did not represent Himself. An apostle does not speak for himself. He has one purpose – to represent another person. An apostle must be completely submitted to another person, that is, Christ, so that he is able to operate in His authority. Jesus said, *"For I did not speak of my own accord, but the Father who sent me commanded me what to say and how to say it."* (John 8:49) That was because He had been made an apostle. He also said, *"For I have come… not to do my will, but to do the will of him who sent me."* (John 6:38) That's an apostle, but that is also a son.

The church needs apostles who are dead to self and who have surrendered everything. These are they who always come representing Christ, never themselves. These are the holy apostles that the church must have. It is from Jesus that we learn what an apostle is. And before Jesus could be made an apostle, He first had to be a son. So the spirit of sonship is always the true foundation of Christian ministry.

It is upon this same building block that we build holy community. And by these graces I look toward the fulfillment, in time, on earth, in various places, of what is spoken of, and will yet come for us: the outworking of Ephesians 2:22:

> *"And in him you too are being built together*
> *to become a dwelling*
> *in which God lives by his Spirit."*

ADDENDUM

TESTIMONIES *of Grace*

FROM MEMBERS OF PEACE APOSTOLIC COMMUNITY

"Every matter must be established by the testimony of two or three witnesses."

2 Corinthians 13: 1

These are living testimonies from a few of our people – some are pastoral leaders, but most are regular members, and generally people I have not asked before to comment. In one case I left in their covering note, since this is also quite revealing of attitudes and relationships, which is our purpose. They are placed in the order in which I received them.

– Author.

From Dr Rhonda Melzer:

Ours is a community full of babies, children and young adults – yet the elderly are cherished and their wisdom respected and sought. The full spectrum of ages is integral to the community and provides a family 'wholeness' that feels right! This is not accidental – it is God's work.

People have hurts and baggage from the past to deal with and experience difficulties, problems, daily struggles and, at times, crises. There is no sense of superiority from others who 'have their act together' or for whom things are 'going smoothly'. It's a community in which we can share our struggles, draw strength, receive Godly council and safely make mistakes! As in a natural family, we are all at different stages of maturity, growth and development; mistakes and challenges are normal – not something to be hidden from other family members.

There is a sense of place and belonging despite the very disparate backgrounds, life experiences (past and present), perspectives and political viewpoints. Forging family with one heart and one mind for his purposes is the Lord's work and is not achieved by anything we do, other than by our asking him to give us a spirit of understanding and a spirit of community…and being willing for him to answer that prayer. It hasn't happened overnight and of course it is a deepening, ongoing process but it is a journey both critical to the life of the Church and the fulfillment of God's purpose locally and on the earth….and it's a fantastic journey to be sharing in.

It is a special thing to watch and share the joys of others in the community – births, marriages, salvation, baptism, physical and spiritual breakthroughs – but perhaps the proof, if any proof was needed, of a real community is the sharing of grief. One of the most profound experiences of God's grace I have ever had occurred recently when the Peace Community, from the very youngest to the oldest, joined together to share in the grief and support of one of our young couples in the loss of their newborn baby. God did something profound amongst us that day; something intangible yet 'solid'. The tears of the young men seemed to me to bear witness to it. The bonds of unity, love, grace and shared community life were both revealed and strengthened through the sharing of such a time and experience.

Before his crucifixion, Jesus prayed to the Father asking that believers would all be one as he and the Father are one and that we would be brought to complete unity thereby revealing the Father's love to the world. And Jesus promised to continue to make the Father known to us that we would be filled with his love. Jesus prayer and promise will be, and is being, fulfilled. I see and experience the tangible evidence of that prayer and promise as God creates community in Peace.

Rhonda Melzer
Manager (Ecological Assessment)
Queensland Parks and Wildlife
Dept Environment and Resource Management
Rockhampton, Qld, Australia.

From Shirley Fisher:

Being in community means so much more than just having what looks like unity as the body of Christ. We need to display the love of Christ. I believe we are genuinely trying to do that. It also means we have a real loving and caring attitude towards our leaders and each other.

It is wonderful to know that when we have a need, be it sickness, a new babe or moving house, we only have to ask and help arrives, meals arrive, or prayers are offered.

Whether we live alone or have family we are part of a larger family that cares for us. This is love - real and genuine and this can only be by the grace of God.

In my Life group of ten ladies we have come to love and care for one another. We were discussing how we had grown together as a people. It was hard to define when things changed, but I believe it started when John publically declared his love for us, and we for him. Something broke and I feel a grace was released.

Many visitors to our church have commented on the love they feel among our people. It isn't always easy to build strong caring relationships with people from different backgrounds and situations, so there has to be a grace present.

When I look around the Church on Sundays I can see people care for one another. It feels so good to be part of this fellowship. I feel truly loved and blessed.

Shirley Fisher,
Cell and Prayer Leader

From John and Elaine Hans:

We have been part of Peace Apostolic Community for over 22 years. We first came to Peace in February 1988. Over the last 22 years we have been active members of the church and have worked in many different ministries within Peace. We have always tried to support John and Hazel Alley and the leadership team in whatever area we could.

Over the years we had grown to know and love the other members of Peace and felt that we had really given our hearts to God and to them, but then God began teaching us about "community". At first we thought we were pretty much going in the right direction with this, because after all we thought this was our desire as well. However, as John began teaching on this subject and sharing with us that it was God's desire to teach us "real community," we realized how little understanding we really had.

God showed us that much of our work was coming from a spirit of independence and competition. In many cases it was obvious that individual ministries within the church were focused on themselves and their success, and there was a feeling that you had to fight for the ministry you were operating in. It was very clear that God wanted us to move into this new sense of community by firstly truly giving our hearts to John and Hazel, and as we did this we found a new security in their love which allowed us to open our hearts more to others in the church.

As a fellowship, God was teaching us to walk with each other in real love. We could see this was true, but no matter what we tried to do to make this happen, we seemed to be going backwards. God showed us that no matter what we did we would never achieve community on our own efforts;

it had to be a move of His Spirit. Instead of trying to find ways of getting together and getting to know each other better, the prayers of the church and individuals turned to seeking God for His grace for community and His anointing for community.

There was recognition that we could get it no other way. It was as though there was a shift from individual praying to corporate praying and seeking God for this move of His Spirit. God answered our prayers and released this grace and anointing and it became more obvious that differences were disappearing and deep love was forming in the relationships within our community. God did a work of grace in our own lives and all independence and competition seemed to drop away. Our focus became more set on Jesus and our church community and less on our own ministries and position.

As we continue to walk in the grace and anointing God has given us, there is a real sense of true community among us as a fellowship. Our love for one another has deepened and our love for God has reached new levels. We look forward to coming together for any reason at all. There is a new truth and depth in the verse that says, 'rejoice with those that rejoice and mourn with those that mourn'. As a fellowship there is now a great desire to move forward together to fulfill the purposes of God…not as individuals, but as a community.

John and Elaine Hans
Founder and Director
Peace International Archery Club

From Marcie Jenkins:

Hi Apostle John!

It has been really wonderful for me to think about how special our church family is and after writing this I am even more grateful for the love and unity in our church. I hope I haven't dribbled on too much and after several attempts, I decided to send this and if you want to use it great and if not that is absolutely fine too. Thanks for the fun of thinking about how wonderful God is in this community of people. God Bless you all the days of your life!

Yours sincerely, Marcie.

In July 2009 Apostle John Alley preached a sermon on Christian Community and challenged us that God had a deeper sense of Community for us to experience in relationships and would we as a people allow God to pour out His Grace on us that we would be of one mind, one heart, to rise as one man to take God's message to the world.

I was so challenged by the spirit of this message, and as a result have taken seriously the question that was asked us on the day of this message, " How much Grace rests on you? Are you willing to seek it in a greater measure?" I went home and asked God for a greater measure of His Grace. As a result the Godly fruit in my life has ripened in the following areas:

1. I have found it very easy to be dedicated to daily prayer and care for the salvation of the people of Rockhampton.
2. I have a deeper unity and intimacy with not only Jesus Christ, but also my family at Peace.
3. I pray more regularly and with a depth of care that I

didn't have so much of before, for the Life group that meets in my home on Thursday nights. I have noticed that the group has grown in its commitment to pray for one another, for the lost, for the ministry and for the city. The unity is sweet and we have moved into a richer level of openness and care and trust with each other.

4. I have found it easier to write worship songs.

5. I have been so encouraged with a deep desire for the first time in years to commit to prayer on Friday nights with the Intercessors of the church. I see this fruit as encouragement that God is anointing his people with Grace and understanding and I have not been left out, we are in this together! Yay!

I admire my family at Peace and I feel very loved and cherished amongst them. I really like the way God has brought us all together and that we came as our Lord led us and we stay because we want to. We are not controlled by man but are submitted to Jesus and one another in the bonds of love. I like that we are not just a bunch of individuals, but that we are joined together by Christ Jesus to form a Team being built up together to be a part of something bigger than ourselves. We are here together to build with Jesus. I am privileged to be a part of the real unity and I not only like the people of Peace but I trust them and love them and share my life, my family and substance with them for the building up of the kingdom and work of God!

Yours sincerely,

Cell Leader

From Carolyn Ponicke:

We at Peace Apostolic Community have been on a journey over the past 10–15 years. The beginning of that journey for me was when John Alley began to preach from the understanding God was giving him with regard to apostolic government in the Church, and how the Church should still function in this way today. As John received further revelation he passed it on to us in thc fcllowship.

So over this period of years we received much teaching on these matters, which included a deeper understanding of 'Pentecost' for us. To put a time and a date on these things would be difficult, but there is no doubt in my mind that at some time in recent years we at Peace have come into community.

As I take the time to think about this I am aware that there is something noticeably different with regard to our relationships with each other at Peace, and this didn't come about in a watershed moment that everyone was aware of, but rather we became aware of it retrospectively. On many occasions visitors would comment that there was 'something' different about us and they felt the love in our midst. This is not something that we have contrived, but rather a grace from the Lord, given to us as we yielded ourselves to the fresh understanding we received.

I know from personal experience that this 'community' we share at Peace is not something I have known anywhere else, nor was it something we shared in my early days at Peace (1991). I believe there is a genuine love shared amongst us. We are concerned for each other. and with regard to the ministry we share one heart and mind and want to see this message carried to all the world.

Worship Leader

From David Hood:

Having been raised in a Christian family which was committed to their local fellowships' program, my view of church life was very much shaped by my experience. I was involved in a denominational-program, performance-based, church life for about 47 years before experiencing what we now describe as relational Christianity.

The releasing of the community anointing that John describes shifted us from being a people who were trying to build relationships through a structural process, to a people who received grace to simply be relational.

For me the big difference is the removal of competition, striving and selfish ambition. When we meet now the atmosphere is very relaxed and sweet, and there is a very real sense of it being OK to be ourselves.

This is still, of course, a work in progress as God continues to deal with us so that Christ can be fully formed in us.

David Hood

Associate Senior Minister
Peace Apostolic Ministries Ltd

From Tony Ponicke:

The people at Peace Apostolic Community have been on a journey now for some 15 years or more. We have had much teaching on the apostolic reformation of the church, and have come to understand the importance of what it means to have apostolic fathers as a foundation in the church today. We have also the great blessing of spiritual sonship, and all the freedoms that come with that revelation – the heart of which is mutual love and honour of each other, and the freedom to do so.

At one point about 8 years ago the church came into a much greater revelation of sonship/community, and we seemed to step into a whole new place of fellowship.

For me, some of the signs were that we, as a people, seemed to strive a lot less; and selfish ambition was much, much less of an issue. There grew amongst us an extremely high regard for the leaders in the church. Our cell groups just seemed to find a better place, and I believe that was the Holy Spirit and the beginning of the anointing of holy community.

At the time I didn't quite grasp what was happening to the whole church, but I knew something was, and there were also huge personal changes happening in my own life.

The things that happened during that time were things that you just can't manufacture. They are not man- made and only grace and anointing from God can change a people like that, and cause it to continue on. I don't believe this grace is fully understood or completely received, but I thank the Lord that it has started.

Pastor
Peace Apostolic Community

From Drs. Brad and Lynda Lorraway:

We deem it an honour and privilege to be part of Peace, having been part of this people for the last 24 years.

Over this period we have seen marked changes in the relationships between people within the church, occurring between the leadership and penetrating to all parts of the body including the children. The major differences we cite include transparency, honesty, accountability, honour and respect of each other, trust and of course love and forgiveness.

The relationships are not superficial, but appear to be built on a deeper love that involves commitment to a common goal and purpose in Christ that overcomes normal relationship hurdles. What is particularly noticeable now is an obvious lack of competition and selfish ambition. Instead, there is a great appreciation and admiration of one another in the role that each is playing in the body and in the potential they have through the grace of God.

We have a freedom to love and respect each other just as we know we are loved and respected by this community, our extended family.

Brad & Lynda Lorraway
Cell Leaders

From Mark Jenkins:

Since God placed my family and I at Peace in 1995 I have seen the fellowship progressively grow in deeper depth of understanding and experience in relating to one another. I do believe God has given us a growing measure of ability to hunger and receive from Him in this way.

It is clear to me we have something very special that is lasting and solid and will continue to build momentum and bring much glory to God.

For me personally, I have been confronted and had to deal with many wrong beliefs and attitudes, especially walking with the leadership of Peace, which has been a journey. In working through these kinds of heart issues I am becoming freer to love and be loved.

I often get taken aback by observing the love, grace and freedom that is reciprocal between the congregation and leadership of Peace. I am appreciative and very happy my family and I are part of Peace Community and look forward to the fulfillment of the many great promises God has given us as a people.

Cell Leader

Other great resources are available FREE

www.peace.org.au

Listen/Download recent messages
Watch video messages
Tune in to Sunday preaching LIVE

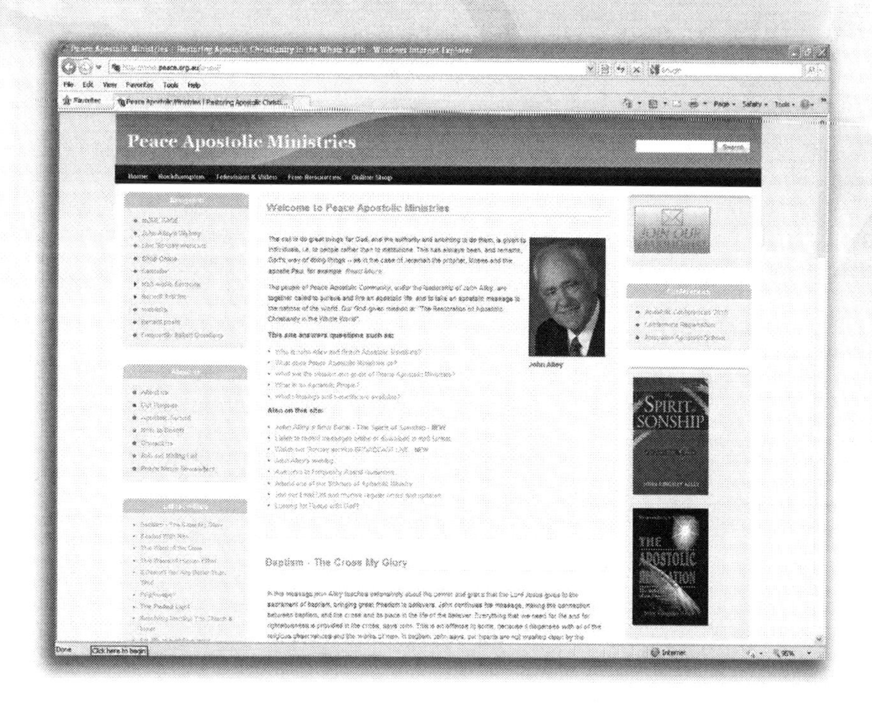

POSTAL ADDRESS:
Locked Bag 8004, Rockhampton QLD 4700, Australia

PHONE: (+617) 4922-7055

EMAIL: mail@peace.org.au
WEB: www.peace.org.au

The Spirit of Sonship

"You are about to glean from a man who's been on an incredible journey of revelation and discovery. I know of no other book published on this subject that is so biblical, inspiring, and practical."
Rev. Dr. John McElroy

The "spirit of sonship" is an apostolic grace which brings about the spiritual maturity of the believer, the revival of apostolic Christianity, and ultimately, the maturity of the church in preparation for the coming of Christ.

This important book reveals that the values and heart attitudes of what we may call the spirit of sonship is the very nature and essence of authentic apostolic New Testament Christianity.

You will discover a fresh approach to understanding and walking in grace, through relationships. The subject is huge, and wonderful; the whole of the Scriptures and all of salvation history must now be seen in the light of *sonship* and its implications.

How to get this resource?

Purchase John Alley's books from
www.shop.peace.org.au

The Apostolic Revelation

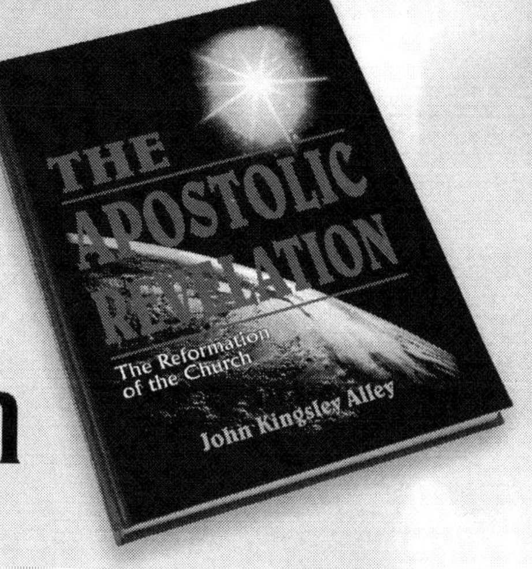

"It is a brilliant book. There is so much biblical content that I would not hesitate to classify it as the premier biblical theology of the apostolic movement..."
C. Peter Wagner

There is an urgency about the message of this book. God has released into the earth a powerful increase of the apostolic and prophetic anointings, and is restoring the apostolic nature of the church itself! Every Christian needs to prayerfully consider the message of this book, and hear what the Spirit is saying to the church. Things are changing, and God is about to act again in history.

The Apostolic Revelation unveils a series of dynamic concepts that are crucial to the life of the church and the restoration of its apostolic power. It establishes benchmarks for the apostolic ministry, and gives definition and substance to the apostolic wineskin of the church. Here is a revelation of apostolic methods, and God's heart for the church and its leadership. In this study, today's apostolic message is harmonised with and grounded in the apostolic revelation of Christ given to Paul, the apostle to the Gentiles. This work is the result of 13 years of inquiry, searching the mind of the Spirit regarding the place of apostles today, and seeking to understand what it means for the church to be the mature apostolic church prepared for the coming of Christ. Apostolic grace is for every believer. This book seeks to equip you to receive a greater grace, and prepare you for the astounding days ahead.

How to get this resource?

Purchase John Alley's books from
www.shop.peace.org.au

Peace Apostolic Ministries

POSTAL ADDRESS:
Locked Bag 8004, Rockhampton QLD 4700, Australia

PHONE: (+617) 4922-7055

EMAIL: mail@peace.org.au
WEB: www.peace.org.au

Made in the USA
Charleston, SC
13 January 2011